AWARENESS HIGH SCHOOL

A Guide to Self Discovery and Mastery
for Students, Teachers, and Parents

BARBARA ABBATE

BALBOA.
PRESS
A DIVISION OF HAY HOUSE

Balboa Press books may be ordered through booksellers or by contacting:

Balboa Press
A Division of Hay House
1663 Liberty Drive
Bloomington, IN 47403
www.balboapress.com
1 (877) 407-4847

Because of the dynamic nature of the Internet, any web addresses or links contained in this book may have changed since publication and may no longer be valid. The views expressed in this work are solely those of the author and do not necessarily reflect the views of the publisher, and the publisher hereby disclaims any responsibility for them.

The author of this book does not dispense medical advice or prescribe the use of any technique as a form of treatment for physical, emotional, or medical problems without the advice of a physician, either directly or indirectly. The intent of the author is only to offer information of a general nature to help you in your quest for emotional and spiritual well-being. In the event you use any of the information in this book for yourself, which is your constitutional right, the author and the publisher assume no responsibility for your actions.

Any people depicted in stock imagery provided by Thinkstock are models, and such images are being used for illustrative purposes only.
Certain stock imagery © Thinkstock.

Print information available on the last page.

ISBN: 978-1-5043-3336-8 (sc)
ISBN: 978-1-5043-3338-2 (hc)
ISBN: 978-1-5043-3337-5 (e)

Library of Congress Control Number: 2015908215

Balboa Press rev. date: 12/16/2015

CONTENTS

Preface ix

Acknowledgments xiii

Chapter 1: Brain Power: How My Mind Can Work For Me 1

Chapter 2: The Paradigm Shift: Paradigm Shifting Is
Like Shape Shifting.. 10

Chapter 3: The Balancing Act: Juggling Mind, Body, and Spirit 19

Chapter 4: Staying Healthy, Staying Fit, Staying Happy................... 27

Chapter 5: Expanding My Boundaries: Seeing Myself
As a Child of the Universe 33

Chapter 6: Walking in Beauty: Honoring Mother Earth 39

Chapter 7: Things Fall Apart: Now What?.................................... 51

Chapter 8: Putting Some Light on the Shadow:
Dealing with the Dark Side 59

Chapter 9: Finding the Power of My Voice: Who Am
I As a Communicator? 67

Chapter 10: Compassion Is the Fashion 75

Chapter 11: Where's the Magic? Seeing the Magic in Science............ 82

Chapter 12: Commencement: Sharing My
Contribution on the Road to Awareness......................... 91

Notes 97

About the Author 101

To Alexis and Cody, the two most important teenagers in my life. They keep teaching me what is real and true about love, forgiveness and compassion.

PREFACE

It's a Friday afternoon at Beach Channel High School in Queens, New York. There are eleven sections of the course Interpersonal Communication in session, and each one of these classes has a sign on the door: Do Not Enter—Guided Fantasy in Session. The students in these classes are taking time to explore their own inner worlds; to discover their innermost dreams and aspirations; and to relax into the power of their own personal potential. The ideas and experiences of this book will give you an opportunity to do the same.

These are the best years of your life. Do you find that hard to believe? When I was a teenager I thought anyone who said that to me was crazy. Yet these are some of the most dynamic years of your life. You are developing at a greater and faster pace than at any other time in your life other than when you were an infant. You have the ability to process and retain more information now than you ever will, and you are in the throes of establishing yourself as an individual who is creating a future of your own design.

The role of any educational system is to provide you with the information and guidance you will need to empower you to make the choices that give you a sense of self and purpose in your life. Despite the focus on academic achievement as measured by standardized testing, there is still work to be done to help you make a connection with what you are learning. Are you equipped to explore what is truly important to you? Do you know how to find what will make you feel fulfilled? Are you learning the skills that you need to succeed in pursuit of your dreams? If you have asked yourself these questions once, twice, or maybe even daily, then you will enjoy the ideas, stories, examples, demonstrations, and exercises outlined in this book.

If you are a teenager on a quest, you might have found this book on your own. Or maybe you are a parent who had an ah-ha moment and seized this book as a tool to assist you in finding the missing link in your child's education. Perhaps you are a teacher looking for an opportunity to try some different techniques in the classroom. Anyone can use the exercises and techniques outlined in this book independently or as part of a group to unlock inner knowing, intuition, and the capacity to connect with what is important to succeed in life. The ideas and lessons presented in *Awareness High School* provide support that you can use throughout your entire life.

The exercises and techniques suggested in *Awareness High School* have been adapted from some originally developed for adults. The work of many great teachers in the human potential movement, masters of mind dynamics, health and well-being practitioners, and communications specialists have been the inspiration for developing a program designed with young readers in mind. *Awareness High School* makes these techniques available to you at a point in your life when it is natural and even imperative to better understand your identity, and how you can make a contribution to the world. Each chapter contains a lesson about a different strategy you can use for your best advantage. Many of the techniques can be used to assist you in any course of study you are now pursuing or in the development of a future vision.

Consider this book as a guide for you on the *road to awareness*, with tools, and insights to open doors for self-discovery, personal empowerment, understanding, and fulfillment. Your journey has the following explorations:

Chapter 1: A study of the brain and how you can use it to uncover what is most important for you to consider in your development.

Chapter 2: The meaning of a paradigm shift, and how we can shift our limiting conversations to conversations that give us power.

Chapter 3: The relationship between your mind, body, and spirit, and the constant dance to balance the three.

Chapter 4: Insights and tips on how to keep yourself in top form physically, mentally, and emotionally.

Chapter 5: An expansion of your vision of who you are and your interconnectedness with all the elements of the universe.

Chapter 6: A look at the connection between you and the planet that sustains you.

Chapter 7: How to maintain your sense of self, inner strength, good will, and forward momentum in the face of setbacks.

Chapter 8: Accepting the shadow side of the personality to gain wisdom and strength.

Chapter 9: Understanding the gift and power of your own voice.

Chapter 10: How compassion arises when you can see all parts of yourself from the weak to the strong, from the dark to the light.

Chapter 11: Seeing the real magic in everything around you. It is with this perception that exploration and discovery occur.

Chapter 12: Your commencement. Aware of yourself and the contributions you want to make to the world, you are ready to set out with confidence on a lifelong journey of awareness.

As with any commencement, graduation from Awareness High School is only a beginning. When you start a journey to become more aware, you open yourself to a life of exploration and learning. It is the most exhilarating path you can take. Awareness of who you are and what is really important to you will be your best guide in remaining on your true path. Here's to your success and fulfillment on this incredible journey.

ACKNOWLEDGMENTS

This book was written out of my love for and commitment to all the young people in my life. I have such a debt of gratitude for all I have learned, all I have encountered, and the sheer joy that I have experienced because of all the marvelous and special beings who have shared a classroom with me. I feel so blessed.

I am thankful for all my teachers, for the Sisters of St. Joseph, who guided me through elementary and high school. I was so lucky to have been at St. Brendan's High School when Sister John Berchmans was principal and John Sexton was our guide in philosophy and academics. I found my art at St. John's with the loving support of Professor Primo Amato, who directed the theatricals. I am grateful to Sam Leiter at Brooklyn College, who guided me to get my license to teach speech in the New York City public schools. If it weren't for him I wouldn't have been qualified to teach at Beach Channel. I bless the day I took the Silva Mind Control course. It propelled me on my journey. I thank God I was able to attend Northwestern University, where I met Dr. Leland Roloff, who changed the way I think; and Anne Thurman, who like an angel directed me to seek employment at the American Conservatory Theatre in San Francisco. I thank Candace Barrett for hiring me to teach at ACT and inspiring me to create a play based on the book *Seven Arrows*. I am so appreciative of all the young actors at ACT's Young Conservatory who helped create that show. I am so glad I met Bill Burnside and Bill Kaunitz in classes at San Francisco State University. They helped me create magic in the show *The Medicine Wheel*. I thank Carl Field, who hired and rehired me to create communications classes at Beach Channel. He had great faith in my ability. I will never forget all the fine young actors at Beach Channel who brought Broadway to the Rockaways. I am so blessed that I had the opportunity to work under the tutelage of Saul Bruckner at Edward R. Murrow High School in Brooklyn. He was a champion in the field of education. I thank my good friend Eileen Newman for always lighting the way for my next step and pointing me in the direction of seeking a position at the Jacqueline Kennedy Onassis High School. There we were able to bring kids from the hood to Broadway. I thank Christine Kloser for all I learned through the Transformational Author Experience. I am ever in gratitude to Eleanore Speert, Judy Rogers, and Susan Valentine for all the initial editing they offered during this book's infancy. I appreciate the women who are a part of my writing group in Austin: Keely Alexander, Susan Burns, Cynthia Garcia, Gretchen Kasting, and Heera Kang. Their kind and encouraging comments have kept me to task.

CHAPTER 1

Brain Power

How My Mind Can Work For Me

Most powerful is he who has himself in his own power.

—Chief Seneca

Have you ever had the experience of being "in the zone?" Everything you did worked out just great. You felt in tune with your surroundings and everything you said came out right. You walked into a room or into your home and you knew all was well. On the other hand, did you ever have one of those days when no matter what you did, it just didn't work out right, or when you walked into your house and you felt immediately that something was wrong? In both cases you felt the vibe, you could feel the energy of what was going on around you, and rightly so. The truth is you can feel the energy around you. You can and do experience the electrical charges in the atmosphere of your surroundings. You might feel that some classrooms you enter are calm and serene, while others are happy and jovial, and then in another the energy might feel unsettling. In this chapter we explore how you can start to become more aware of this energy, identify it, and even manage it for your best advantage. The first step is to become aware.

What is awareness? Where does our awareness dwell? How do I know what I know? How do I decide what is important for me to know and what is important for me to do? Who is the one who wants to know, and who is the one asking these questions? Is it that little voice inside of me, and where

1

does that little voice come from? In the following chapters we will take a journey together on the *road to awareness* to answer these questions and discover what those answers will mean for your growth and development.

In this first chapter we will explore the way your brain functions. You will come to understand that your brain is a powerful instrument that gives off various electrical currents or brain waves. You will be able to identify those different brain waves and come to understand that your brain really is like a computer. You have the ability to program your brain like a computer to think, and consequently affect your behavior in ways that are most beneficial for you. You will learn ways to use certain brain waves to your best advantage.

Awareness means "having or showing realization, perception, or knowledge." Let's begin our journey on the road to awareness. The purpose of the stories, examples, and demonstrations in this chapter is to illustrate how brain power can be used to gain insights and answers when traditional thinking is not yielding the needed solutions. We will explore how these brain game techniques can be incorporated into your journey.

In 1972, I had the day off for Flag Day, which was a school holiday in Brooklyn and Queens. I turned on the TV, which I rarely got a chance to watch in the mornings, and watched the *Today Show*. A priest by the name of Father Barum was being interviewed about a course he was teaching called Silva Mind Control. I was impressed by what he had to say about the results people were achieving by using the techniques that were taught in the course. People were saying they were able to be more productive; they were able to easily find things they had lost; and that they were doing better in school or on their jobs. I quickly wrote down all the information and immediately called to register. I took myself to the McAlpin Hotel on West Thirty-Fourth Street that following weekend, where the course was being offered.

There were at least three hundred people in the large ballroom at the McAlpin Hotel where the Silva Mind Control Course was being presented. We were all there to learn the techniques of the Silva Method, which were developed by Jose Silva. The techniques involved learning to understand

and control the electrical frequencies emitted by the human brain. By becoming more aware of the more productive frequencies, one can become more in control of his or her life.

Jose Silva was fascinated by the transmission of radio waves. He understood that the human brain acts in a similar fashion by transmitting different frequencies. He did experiments to measure, calculate, and determine the effects of human brain wave transmission. He saw that the brain transmits different frequencies under various conditions. While awake, the brain operates under a *Beta* frequency, 14–21 cycles per second. These frequencies are measured in Hz, named after Heinrich Hertz, who demonstrated that electromagnetic energy exists and can be detected and measured. Electromagnetic radiation is all around us. The waves range from high-frequency cosmic and gamma rays through X-rays, ultraviolet light, infrared radiation, and microwaves, down to very low frequency radio waves. The brain frequencies emitted by the human brain can be designated in the following way:

The more relaxed, in-tune frequency of light sleep and meditation is called *Alpha*, which is a lower brain frequency at 7–14 Hz.

During deep sleep the brain frequency is at *Theta* from 4–7 Hz.

Finally, when the brain is in deep sleep, a coma, or sometimes in a deep trance experienced by some yogis, the brain frequency is at *Delta* at 0–4 Hz.

Through his own experimentation, especially with his own children, Jose Silva discovered that the mind is highly suggestible while at the more in-tune Alpha level. By utilizing some of the techniques he developed, his subjects became more productive, creative, skillful, and even clairvoyant, meaning they were able to see beyond the range of ordinary perception.

According to Jose Silva, the more you practice the techniques required to get into the Alpha level, the better you will be at using the Alpha state to attain the things you want. One technique was the *three-finger* technique, using an anchor, simply putting your thumb, index, and middle fingers together. *Anchor* is a hypnosis term that refers to a simple physical activity you can use to help you achieve a particular result. Some people might put their hand over their heart when they want to calm down. According to Jose Silva, by simply putting your three fingers together you can bring your brain waves to an Alpha level and then simply tell yourself what it is that you might want. You could put a suggestion into your mind for anything from finding a parking space to getting a good mark on an exam. An important aspect of this technique is that you will be able to suggest to yourself only those things that will be good for you and others. Over time, by using these techniques you will start to see results. This became a handy little trick I used to find parking spots while living in New York City. I also discovered that my anxiety level would drop if I simply put my three fingers together during a tense situation.

Another important tool is the ability to use your *mental screen*, which is your ability to use your imagination to see images in your mind. When I learned how to do it, I was a young teacher at PS 42, a very old public school in the Arverne neighborhood of Queens, New York. The school was poorly equipped, missing desks, chairs, and books. The classes were overcrowded. I started to use some of the Silva Method techniques with my students, who were seven years old. The idea was to help them relax and to be more in control of themselves.

Around the same time, the school received a grant for a cultural enrichment program called Cultural Opportunities in the Metropolitan Environment (COME). I had the opportunity to take many of the children in the school to a variety of cultural programs, including a production of *Our Town* by Thornton Wilder. The culmination of the program was a theatrical production created by the students. We based our performance on *The Me Nobody Knows: Children's Voices from the Ghetto*, edited by Stephen M. Joseph, using original poetry and pieces written by the children at PS 42 themselves. It was then that we started to experiment with adaptations of the techniques I had learned from the Silva Method. We would all stand in a circle, close our eyes, and imagine that light was filling our bodies from our heads to our toes. We would then imagine that this light turned different colors. One child would stand in the middle and tell us the color of light they felt they wanted for that day, depending on their mood or their needs. Using their imaginations the children in the circle would beam that color of light to the child in the center of the circle. One of the boys in that group later created a dance company called Purple Light from his remembrance of that exercise he had done as a child. Another student from that group later appeared on Broadway in *Dream Girls*, directed by Michael Bennett.

I was teaching elementary school at the time but wanted to teach theatre on the high school level. I realized I needed to get a masters degree in theatre and communications in order to be qualified to do that. I had no idea where I would go or how I would proceed. The Silva Method teaches a technique that addresses this kind of circumstance, when you really do not have a clear picture of a solution or the outcome you would like. It is the *glass of water* technique, and I must say it is my favorite. Simply drink half a glass of water before going to sleep at night, and say to yourself as you look upward, "This is all I have to do to solve the problem I have in mind." Do the same in the morning with the remaining water. It is recommended that you stay alert for a period of seventy-two hours for your answer to appear in the form of a sign or symbol. I did the exercise on a Sunday, and the next day I had an appointment at Brooklyn College. I was an hour early, so I went to the library to check out college bulletins. There were none that interested me on the library shelves; however there was a note that said other bulletins would be in room 207. I went to that room. It was an office with a desk, bookshelves, and a long reading table. On the top shelves were computer printouts, and the bottom shelves were dedicated to college bulletins. The odd thing was that on the inch shelving that separated the two was my name taped to the shelf: BARBARA. Right under my name was the bulletin for Northwestern University. I opened the bulletin and realized that this was the school for me.

Soon after that discovery, I learned that the whole area where I was teaching was going to be turned into the first urban national park, called Gateway National Park. The federal government was going to help fund the building of a new high school of oceanography. I applied to be the drama teacher when the school would open the following year. I was accepted for this position. I could earn my masters at Northwestern in Evanston, Illinois, and then return to teach at the school.

This was a dream come true. Many of the students I had taught at PS 42 would then be my students at the new high school. This school was to be the High School of Oceanography. Part of the mission of this new magnet school was to support the efforts of the rangers of the national park in cleaning up Jamaica Bay. The students from PS 42 would be going to a brand new, beautifully equipped school situated right on Jamaica Bay. At this school they would have the opportunity to learn scuba diving so they could better explore the marine samples in Jamaica Bay. I was to be a teacher in the Communication Arts Department, where I would teach drama, public speaking, interpersonal communication, and broadcasting—subjects that would give these students a whole different way to navigate in their lives.

Over a period of one year, the children of PS 42 and I used the Alpha conditioning techniques. Many opportunities opened up for us, and wonderful things started to emerge. These techniques can be used to help you identify things you would like to change in your life and to open you to beneficial ways to achieve the goals that will assist you in making those changes.

The following activity is a technique for creating and using your own mental screen, useful when you want to program beneficial outcomes for situations in your life.

Try This for Yourself

- Sit quietly, feet flat on the floor, hands on your lap, and gaze at a point in front of you about forty-five degrees above the horizon line. Start counting down from ten to one, slowly.

- Say each number in your head and see if you can see each number as they may appear on a large TV screen as on *Sesame Street*.

- With each descending number take a deep, long breath, inhaling slowly and exhaling in the same rhythm.

- When you reach the number one, see in your mind's eye that you are in a very comfortable place anywhere in the world. It could be on top of a mountain, or even beneath the sea, just as long as you know it is a wonderful place where you can feel the most powerful.

- When there, imagine that there is a large easy chair where you can sit. Before you is a large screen. This is your mental screen where you can see the past, the present, or the future.

- Place on your mental the screen an image of something that may be troubling you or that you would like to change. Put a colored light around the frame and let the image pass to the left.

- Now put an image of the way you would like the scene to unfold, or how you would like the situation to turn out. Put a white light around that. This is the image you can revisit at any time when you want to energize the positive outcome you are wishing to achieve. According to Laura Silva of Silva International your imagination is stronger than your will power in supporting you in affecting positive changes in your life.

- Count from one to five to yourself, open your eyes, and feel better than before and more refreshed.

- Whenever you want to imagine that situation, put in your mind only the way you saw it with the white light. See what happens over a period of time.

I used these techniques when I was a student at Northwestern. There were times that I used the three-finger technique while studying and taking tests. These techniques helped me to clarify what to study for my exams. They also helped me understand better what my professors were looking for in the projects they assigned.

What does this mean for you?

If your mind works like a computer and you can program it to support you in determining, taking action steps, and achieving your goals, then why not learn some techniques that will assist you in taking control of your mind? Why not learn ways to set up images in your mind that will assist you to achieve what you want for your life? Using some of the techniques that have been suggested in this chapter may offer you some support.

At first, practice going to an Alpha level by using the method described in this chapter. Count down from ten to one to achieve a more relaxed state. Then try using some of the techniques suggested such as:

- The *anchor:* putting your three fingers together, or covering your heart with your hand;

- The *mental screen:* to work out solutions for problems or projects that you have by visualizing solutions.

See what results you are able to produce for yourself.

Try some of these techniques in your classes at school. If you have a class that is particularly difficult for you, sit in class with your three fingers together and just say to yourself, "I will understand and know everything that is taught." See if this helps. Then work with these techniques on larger issues and questions to improve control of your brain power. Good luck.

CHAPTER 2

The Paradigm Shift
Paradigm Shifting Is Like Shape Shifting

> *Within you right now is the power to do things you*
> *never dreamed possible. This power becomes available*
> *to you just as soon as you can change your beliefs.*
>
> —*Maxwell Maltz*

When I was sixteen years old, I went to see a production of *Six Characters in Search of an Author*, a play by Luigi Pirandello, at the McAlpin Theatre (the same place where I took the Silva Mind Control course, a funny coincidence). I was very moved by the staging of the play, but I was particularly struck by the message it portrayed. The play starts with the cast and crew of a play assembling for a rehearsal. Just as the rehearsal begins, the lights in the theatre grow dim, and eerily, six characters, oddly clothed and with heavy make-up, seem to float in as a group onto the stage. The six characters are looking for a director. Each one tells his or her version of the story they want produced as a play. Unfortunately, there can be no play, because each character tells a different version of the story.

When I returned to the Thirty-Fourth Street subway station after the show, I had a moment of reflection, and my first true *epiphany:* "an unusually sudden manifestation or perception of the essential nature or meaning of something" according to Merriam–Webster. I realized from the theme elaborated in the play that everyone has an individual perception of reality.

Your view of life can only be an illusion of what is real because it is defined by the limitation of what you see, and how you perceive. Consequently, there is no single view of reality, only millions of interpretations. I realized that my mother and father had their own views of reality, as did everyone standing on that subway platform. At that moment I realized that I create my own reality and that I can be conscious of creating the reality that best suits me. I was deeply moved by that understanding. It was the play *Six Characters in Search of an Author* that helped me to understand that concept. I saw how powerful theatre can be. It was then that I knew my life would be dedicated to that art form.

The Paradigms Through Which We See the World

A *paradigm* is "a philosophical or theoretical framework of any kind." How we see the world is colored by our upbringing, our families, our surroundings, our beliefs, our culture, our language, our ethnic and racial ties, our schooling, and our friends. All of these influences help to create the frames through which we see the world. Sometimes these beliefs can be extremely helpful, and at other times they may limit our growth. Often these beliefs are held within us in the form of conversations we have with ourselves about the nature of reality and how we see things. These conversations influence our behavior. It is in these moments that we get to choose the conversations that will be the most beneficial for us. We do have the power to shift these belief systems, and to change the course of our behavior and our lives if we see that a certain conversation regarding what we think we believe about ourselves does not serve us. This is what is meant by a *paradigm shift*.

We are dominated by our habitual conversations about who we are, and about what we can or cannot do. Many of these conversations are based on early interpretations about what is real. Just think for a moment about the possibility that some of the beliefs that you hold to be true are true only because you make them so, or you were told that they are so. The way we act in certain situations is determined by our internal conversations. Remember that little internal voice we talked about in chapter 1? How we respond to those conversations is an act of *will*. "Will I" or "Will I not" do something is determined by your willpower. The idea is to be able to look at those internal conversations and see whether they are helpful or harmful.

One inner conversation I realized was running a big portion of my life throughout high school and college was the conversation, "I'm always in the wrong place at the wrong time." I even had my friends convinced of the truth of this conversation. It became funny when things would go wrong while I was around. Fingers could point to me as the source of the misfortune. I realized that this was not a very empowering way to go through life, so I thought about changing that internal conversation to something that would help me instead of harm me. Changing a conversation of this sort is what is known as a *paradigm shift*. You are changing a belief system that has become embedded in your mind. This takes the power of your will. I changed my disempowering conversation to an empowering one: "I will be in the right place at the right time." Then I started to operate out of that new conversation, that new paradigm. Lo and behold, my circumstances started to shift, and more often than not, I found myself in amazing and wonderful situations. My new internal conversation allowed me to perceive more enlivening opportunities.

Many of the students I had taught in the elementary school in Arverne, Queens, had no idea that they lived between the Atlantic Ocean and Jamaica Bay. When they were little I used to take them on the subway from Rockaway to Manhattan. Each child was given a subway map so they could track our route. They could see all the bridges, waterways, boroughs, and neighborhoods we would travel across as we rode into Manhattan. When Beach Channel High School opened, these students were given a whole new perspective on life. Their view of the world was expanded, and a shift occurred in what they saw as available to them. Their world was not narrow, as the discovery of all the world's oceans became a part of their study. They were given the chance to participate in a dynamic paradigm shift on an environmental level. Their world view was broadened.

Beach Channel was the first school of oceanography in New York City. The students were to work with the Coast Guard and the rangers at the National Park to clean up Jamaica Bay, which was considered a dead zone at the time. The students learned scuba diving and accompanied the rangers to test the water and retrieve marine samples from the islands in Jamaica Bay that were leased to the school by New York City. The students helped the rangers build nesting grounds for birds. This area had always been a major migratory route for birds. After the school opened, in a period of less than ten years, over ten species of birds returned to the area, including Arctic terns, skimmers, wild swans, egrets, herons, and even pelicans. I saw a flock of baby pelicans fly above my head as I swam in the waters very near Beach Channel. The students helped to create this paradigm shift in an area that was considered dead.

When I lost my job at Beach Channel because of a New York City budget crunch, my new personal paradigm was being challenged. I could see this as an opportunity to experience myself in the right place at the right time rather than being at a loss. I wrote to one of my professors at Northwestern. She recommended that I apply for a position at the American Conservatory Theatre in San Francisco, which had an opening for a drama coach and director in their Young Conservatory program. I applied for the job and was invited to ACT for an interview. I knew that working at ACT would be a great thing. I knew I was in the right place at the right time. I wound up teaching at the American Conservatory Theatre in San Francisco under the direction of Bill Ball. It was Bill Ball who had directed that production of *Six Characters in Search of an Author* at the McAlpin Theatre, which altered the direction of my life.

Years later, I had the opportunity to teach at Edward R. Murrow High School in Brooklyn. The principal at the time was Saul Bruckner. He believed that the more freedom you give students, the more they will choose responsibility. At Murrow there were no bells and no hall passes. Students had a free period every day, separate from lunch, called an *OPTA Band* to do anything they wanted, including hanging out with their friends in the halls. There might be 1500 students hanging out in the halls each period. Classes were non-graded so that freshmen, sophomores, juniors, and seniors could all elect to take the same classes. It was a pass–fail system with no grades, and students were not penalized if they elected to cut a class. You may ask if there was pandemonium in the school. The answer is no. Murrow has one of the highest college entrance rates in all of New York City and operates to this day on Mr. Bruckner's principles.

I was the coordinator of the TV studio, so I had many students hanging out and working on projects throughout the day. One student was complaining that he never passed math. I explained that he had a conversation that he never passed math, and he said, "That's right, I never pass math." I said, "No, it's only a conversation you have. Are you willing to give up that conversation?"

He thought about it for a moment, and I convinced him he had nothing to lose. I asked him to sit and relax and to count down from ten to one as you did in chapter 1. Then he brought the conversation to mind: "I can't pass math." He let that dissolve from his mind, then brought to mind the opposite conversation: "I can pass math." He put a bright light around that. As he refocused on his present surroundings, I recommended that he hold the new thought in his mind as often as he could. He went on his way.

A week passed, and he came back into the TV studio and threw a math paper onto my desk with a mark of 92. He exclaimed, "I can pass math!" Years after he graduated he came back to visit me and said that he was working on Wall Street for some brokers. They were using him to track and pick stocks. He said he became very good at picking winners and used the technique he had learned in shifting his own conversation around his inability to pass math. See what a little paradigm shift can do?

Now what does this mean for you?

Take a look at the disempowering conversations you have that do not support you. Your conversations might be among the following:

I can't do_____

I'm not good at_____

I will never be able to_____

I won't ever have enough of_____

I bet you can think of some conversations that bother you at night, or early in the morning when you are just waking, that you would like to shift. A new way of behaving is only a conversation away.

· Relax as you did in chapter 1. Sit quietly and count down from ten to one in the same way you did before.

· This time when you are in your special place of power, bring to mind a conversation that you have that does not support you. Let it pass to the left.

· Now bring to mind a shift in that conversation that would be more empowering. Put a bright light around that conversation and then let the image dissolve.

· Count up again from one to five and open your eyes.

· Bring the new conversation to mind whenever you get a chance and see what results you get.

What do you do when a conversation doesn't seem to take hold or doesn't always work when you need it?

Like with any skill, it takes practice. Keep repeating empowering conversations, sentences, and mantras over and over again until your brain accepts the message and you reap the benefits.

There are times when I feel that my emotions are running through my body and causing me to react as if a flash flood of feelings is sweeping me away in the momentum of an upsetting or unsettling situation. Emotions are energy in motion and you certainly feel them throughout your body. It is at those times that you are called on to use your will to harness your breath in an attempt to gain back equilibrium. A friend of mine starts to say the alphabet to find a word that will bring healing or soothing or power in the moment of upset. A-accept, B-breathe, C-calm, D-delight she mentally repeats until she finds the word that brings her calm. It may work as well as counting to ten to let your brain calm down to open to an appropriate response. Focusing on discovering peace and calm in any situation can assist you in discovering the best actions to take to achieve success for yourself.

Practice Quick Paradigm Shifts

In moments when you are experiencing irritation, annoyance, or some minor upset, take a moment and close your eyes.

- Try to relax your eyes and the area around your eyes, and behind your eyes.

- Then relax your ears and the area around your ears and inside your ears.

- Open your eyes and see what is good; hear what is enlivening or pleasant in the environment right now.

- Shift your energy and attitude about the situation from frustration to peace or from annoyance to acceptance.

- Put yourself in a bubble of light and transmit that light to the space around you. See if you experience more calm or peace about how you relate to what previously might have set you off balance.

Practicing this ability in instances of minor upheaval gives you strength to use this skill when situations get really tough and there is a need for you to shift your perceptions from a losing reality to one in which you win.

Sometimes there are conversations that you want to nurture and develop, conversations that give you a sense of power and pride. It is important to pay attention to those, too. When my son was three years old, we were driving in the car. As he was gazing out the back window, he blithely said, "Mommy, I have a crystal ball in my brain." Having a crystal ball in one's brain can be a very useful image.

I encouraged this idea by saying, "You absolutely do, and how lucky you are to have one!" He is now seventeen, and to this day I remind him of that conversation and prompt him to use that idea to his advantage. Any person who can use a crystal ball to determine the future can set himself up with the image that can support his own ability to do just that.

What conversations do you have that support you and your growth?

Make a list of things you say to yourself that are useful and encouraging that can be used as your own personal mantras.

Create a saying or a slogan that will spur you to achieve what you want in the world.

Here's to some good conversations.

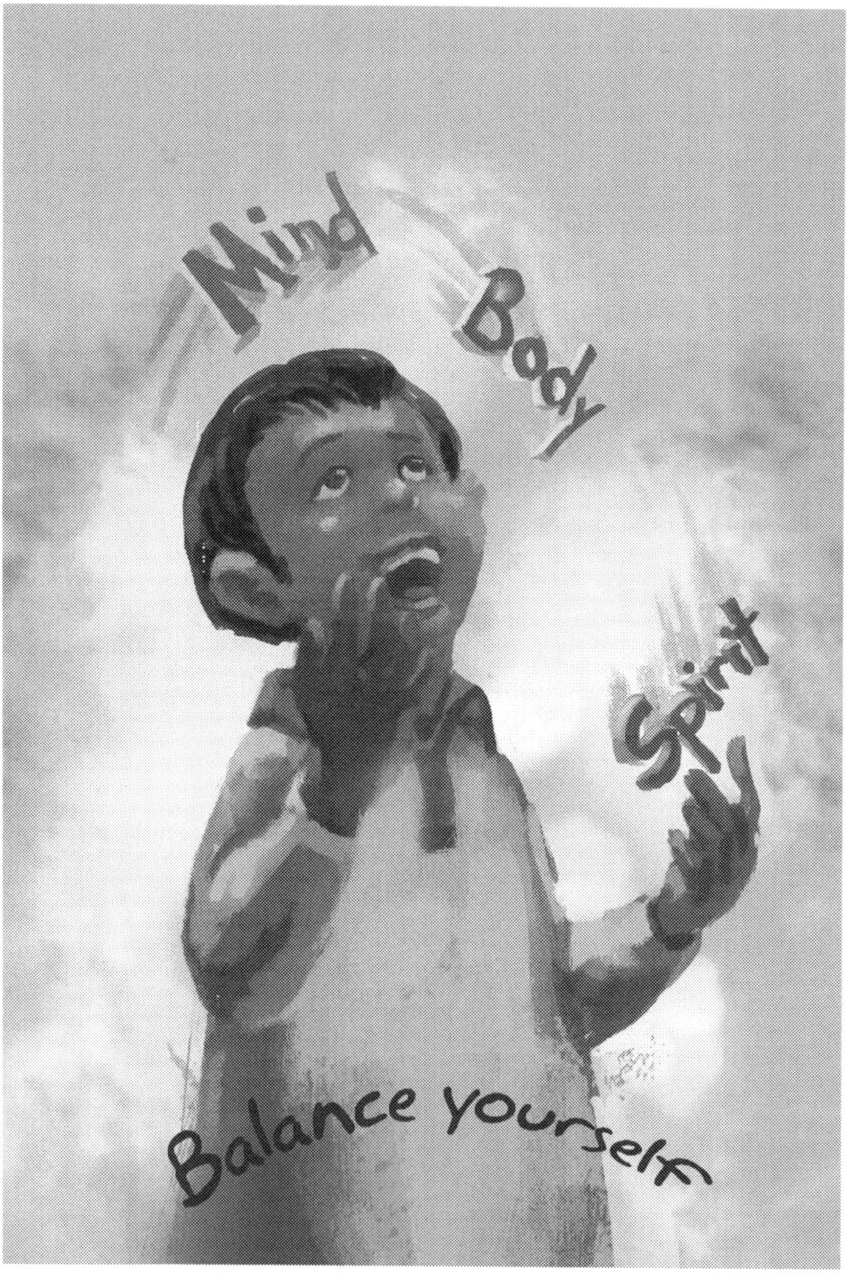
Mind
Body
Spirit
Balance yourself

CHAPTER 3

The Balancing Act
Juggling Mind, Body, and Spirit

Whether you think you can, or think you can't, you're right.

—Henry Ford

Your thoughts influence your health and your emotional states. You have thousands of thoughts a day. Your mind never stops, even when you are sleeping. You are continually talking to yourself, and most of the time you are not even aware of what you are saying. Those thoughts that are running through your mind have an influence on your emotions, your spirit, and ultimately your health. The way you manage those thoughts is the key to who and what you want to be in your life. This is where true mastery begins.

The first step is to start paying attention to your thoughts. What are you saying to yourself? It's a bit like paying attention to the little angel or devil you've seen sitting on a cartoon character's shoulder, telling him what to do. Daily, a barrage of conversations plays a continual loop in your brain. Just noticing them at first is a big step. "I'm tired." "I'm hot." "I'm cold." "I hate him." "I like her." "That teacher drives me nuts, I'm so bored." And so on. It's an endless stream of thoughts in your head. This is the beginning of awareness.

Once you become aware of these thoughts, you can start to see that there is a relationship between the thoughts you have and the emotions you experience. "Here comes that girl (or boy) I like." "I forgot to do an important assignment that's due today." "I'll never make the team." All these thoughts give rise to a varying array of emotions. You may feel anxious, agitated, angry, fearful, upset, hurt, calm, or happy. Dr. Joe Dispenza in his book *Breaking the Habit of Being Yourself* provides insights into how the brain functions and how thoughts create chemical reactions within the body. Your thoughts release certain chemicals called *neuropeptides* into your bloodstream. These neuropeptides attach to certain cells in your body, and before you know it you are feeling great—or not so great, depending on the thoughts you are having. Over a period of time, if you habitually have the same thought that produces a negative emotion, the cells in your body become conditioned to that response and begin to anticipate and actually crave that chemical stimulus. Some people become habitually sad, angry, victimized, fearful, or tense because they have given the cells in their bodies an overdose of the chemicals associated with those emotions. Now the cells begin to crave those chemical blasts. It becomes a vicious circle of thought, chemical release associated with that thought, and the emotional response. The emotion has become an addiction.

Cells that are bombarded by the onslaught of such negative emotions become weakened and as such become susceptible to disease. There is a direct correlation between the thoughts you have, the emotions you experience, and the health of your body. Cells that are constantly attacked by the chemicals released by negative emotions do not receive the nutrients necessary for their development, and become stressed.

How can you balance all of that? How can you insure that your cells are receiving the appropriate nutrients? The key is that you have control over your thoughts. Thousands of thoughts bombard the mind each day. When you become adept at noticing your thoughts, you can then observe the effect that the thought or thoughts have on your emotions and your body. The next step is to train your mind to replace those thoughts that are negatively affecting you with a thought that will give you power and control over what you want to be feeling and doing instead. Like any skill, this takes some practice.

You may see this as a form of positive thinking, but more accurately, it is a process that allows you to interrupt habitual stimulus-response reactions by cutting off the stream of chemicals that keep them in place. Once you have associated a particular thought with a particular emotion, you can create a thought that will enable you to interrupt that pattern. This technique is called *reframing*. You literally give your mind a different picture of a negative situation to focus on. It's a bit like creating a better ending to a movie or story to achieve a better outcome.

Let's say you have a friend who is not being nice to you. This behavior continues, so that every time you see, hear about, or even think about this person, you feel sad, hurt, betrayed, angry, or maybe all of these emotions at once. Over time these feelings will become imprinted on you to the point where the emotions take over how you respond or act around this individual. What if you said to yourself, "I am feeling hurt, angry, sad," or whatever the feeling may be? "I am letting that feeling run me." "I am powerful enough to replace that thought with the thought that I am strong, powerful, happy, accepting, or understanding." Whether it is the actual occurrence, or the memory of that situation, you will release the same chemicals to produce the same reaction. Replacing a disempowering thought with an empowering thought sends a different chemical message throughout your body and energizes rather than debilitates your cells and ultimately you.

There are myriad ways any situation can turn out. All around you are bits of information and knowledge that can lead you in a thousand different directions. You are the observer, the chooser, the healer, the creator, the captain and the guide of your destiny. When you limit your thoughts and reactions to memory, habitual ways of responding, or by conditioned behaviors, you limit the possibilities and potentials that are available. You can reframe situations in your life so that you can guarantee a more productive or harmonious outcome for yourself. *Reframing* is a technique that allows you to create a more positive interpretation or story line around a situation that may be bothering you.

Your life is an opportunity to explore and discover daily the countless miracles and mysteries that are right in front of you. Your thoughts are powerful. Your thoughts are aspects of your imagination, your image-making ability. This ability to create images in your mind gives you power. Nothing in the world is etched in stone. The molecules that comprise what you think of as solid are in motion around empty space. In many ways you are conditioned to see only what you have been trained to see, so that often you miss much of what is actually around you. At other times you are very selective about what you see. Have you ever had the experience when someone told you of a new item that was on the market that you never heard of before, and then you immediately start to see it everywhere?

The "who" you present to the world is represented through your body. You may think that no one is noticing what you are feeling or thinking, but the truth is other people see many things about you through the way you use your body to move around in the world, by the energy you transmit, by the emotions you express, by your vocal tones, and by the words you choose. You are your own instrument, and it is through you that your song is played, and the dance of your life is performed.

As part of a creative writing class, students at Beach Channel High School prepared *body poems* to look at some of these aspects of themselves. We took large sheets of brown postal wrapping paper and cut it to the size of each student. Each student lay down, and a classmate traced that student's outline on the sheet. Each student was given a selection of different colored pencils and knelt down in front of their outlined forms. Then they responded to various statements by drawing images, words or phases on the various parts of their body form.

Some of the statements were:

The right side of my body says ...

The left side of my body says ...

It hurts when I think of ...

I hold back here ... when ...

My hearts says ...

Dreams flow through me ...

Thoughts fill my mind ...

What I don't say ...

The color I most feel inside is where ...

My right hand expresses ...

My left hand expresses ...

Please make up a few statements of your own.

Each student had a visual body poem depicting many of the thoughts, images, emotions and feelings that they held within themselves. The body poems were placed around the room as a visual display of the students' inner dialogues, experiences, feelings and attitudes. They became an inspiration for writing assignments we did later in the term. The body poem is a wonderful way to look inside yourself to see what thoughts, feelings and images are within you and where you experience those in your body. Some you may want to release, some you may want to explore, others you may want to nurture. Becoming aware of your internal dialogues, feelings, emotions, thoughts, and images is a part of the process of self-discovery along the road to awareness.

Your thoughts affect your relationship to your environment, your emotional states, and your health. Consciousness is the awareness of the power that you have over your thoughts. Dr. Masaru Emoto, in his book *The Hidden Messages of Water*, explains how water molecules react to certain expressions of energy. When words and thoughts such as "I love you" or "Thank you" were directed to the water, the molecules arranged themselves in beautiful crystal patterns resembling snowflakes. When thoughts such as "I hate you" or "You make me sick" were directed to the water, the molecules became chaotic and muddy looking.

I was working as a part of Project Hope in the Catskill Mountains after the ravages of Tropical Storm Irene. The Schoharie Creek normally meanders through the area in a peaceful and calming way; however, during this storm it became extremely destructive and destroyed several towns. Some Native American healers were brought to Prattsville, which had incurred the brunt of the storm's devastation, to send loving thoughts and kind words to bring healing to those waters. You are composed of more than 60 percent water. The thought that energy directed at you, or that you generate within yourself might affect the patterning of your cells is something to consider.

Meditating is one of the best ways to keep your mind, body, and soul in good condition. It is a method of slowing down your mind using simple awareness of your breath. The relaxation techniques we discussed in chapter 1 are a forms of meditation. Evidence suggests that in some cases the regular practice of meditation can give people the ability to heal ailments in their own bodies, such as digestive conditions, heart ailments, respiratory concerns, and problems brought on by anxiety or stress.

Deepak Chopra is a medical doctor and one of the world's leading proponents of the effectiveness of mindfulness in self-healing. In his book *Power, Freedom, and Grace* he states, "Imagine that your nervous system is the hardware, and all the chemical changes that occur in your body are the software. The software, or program, changes according to your thoughts, feelings, interpretations, and desires. But there is a programmer. Who is the programmer? The programmer is the inner self, the silent witness, the ever-present awareness that witnesses everything. And when you get in touch with the silent witness, this gives you the ability to rewrite the program. To become familiar with the miracle of the human body-mind is to acquire awesome power."

What is that power? It is the power to generate peace and well-being within yourself.

What You Can Do

There are many methods for producing this effect.

The simplest is to concentrate on your breathing, both when you inhale and when you exhale. This slows down your heart rate and your brain frequency, as we saw in chapter 1.

Count backward from ten to one, or repeat a simple phrase like "I can feel my heart rate slowing down."

A method I use to become more aware of my breath is to imagine that I have a regulator button that scuba divers use to control their oxygen levels, and consequently their buoyancy. I press an imaginary button with my thumb to allow my breath to become deeper so that I can feel more buoyant or relaxed.

Your breath is the most powerful tool at your disposal for giving you the control to soothe your own mind, body, and spirit. Deep breathing is a tool you can use to heal yourself. You switch the frequencies in your brain to produce a more healing effect. You have control over your well-being so that you can be a well being. Calming yourself through meditation or any similar sort of breathing exercise connects you to what Carl Jung, a famous psychologist, calls the "collective unconscious." Dr. Leland Roloff, a professor of mine at Northwestern, called it the underground stream that connects us all. This underground stream is where the still waters of your intuition reside. It is where you will find that wise inner voice that can give you guidance. Going back to the idea that the human body is composed of 60 percent water, calming those waters with soothing words may have a similar effect on the cells in your body as the messages sent to water during Dr. Emoto's experiments. "Lead me to still waters," as expressed in many prayers, may be a return to your inner center, where the still waters of your inner wisdom dwell.

CHAPTER 4

Staying Healthy, Staying Fit, Staying Happy

As human beings imbued with free will, we can use the power of our consciousness to re-create our reality; including but not limited to a body, mind and spirit free of disease.

—*Sol Luckman*

Staying healthy is a lifelong commitment. You have seen how your thoughts influence your health. The next important thing to consider is the care of the body you have been given. It is precious, it is vulnerable, and it does deteriorate. It is the vessel that contains everything that is essential for your life. How you feed it, water it, nourish it, exercise it, and rest it will have a lasting influence on its ability to perform to the level you desire. Some people take better care of their animals or even their plants than they do their own bodies.

You really do know what your body needs. You have been told and warned by your parents and teachers to eat healthy, drink lots of water, stay away from junk food, eat healthy snacks, and exercise to stay fit. You know the benefits of exercise and proper sleep habits. Then why don't you do what you know is best for you? Is it because you do not believe that there will be consequences if you ignore the advice you get on ways to stay healthy? Or perhaps you see the advice as good only for adults who have already made a mess of themselves?

It is hard to stay healthy in our culture. You are bombarded by hundreds of ads on TV, radio, and the social media to buy foods that are not good for you. You are being enticed to crave foods that will damage not only your health, but the health of the planet. You are conditioned to crave breakfast cereals that will drain you of energy and overload your system with sugars that provide very little nutrition. The amount of high fructose corn syrup that is in most processed foods and soft drinks can be damaging. These foods are manufactured to be very appealing. You become so conditioned to the tastes of these products, which are loaded with salt, sugar, and chemicals, that you become accustomed to these tastes and crave them more and more. It's a vicious cycle and you are the pawn.

The health of American teens is deteriorating. There is an epidemic of childhood and teen obesity. Fast food chains that cater to teens' tastes are big business in this country and around the world. How can you resist the allure of this constant barrage of misinformation about what you should put into your body? The subtext of the commercials for these fast foods is actually the message to eat or drink as much as you can no matter how bad it may be for you. There are so many artificial ingredients, preservatives, and chemicals in many packaged foods that we run the risk of becoming an artificial species if we continue to use them as a substitute for what is truly nutritious. Do you feed your body the foods that will give it the proper fuel to enhance your well-being; keep you fit and nourished; and supply you with the energy to help you maintain your physical, emotional, and mental determination and will power?

Just as you have control over thoughts that affect your emotional states and well-being, you have control over what you put in your mouth. Exercising care over what you eat also is an act of will and of determination to keep yourself fit and in good shape. Get in the habit of reading labels. You will be surprised by the number of chemicals and the amount of sugar, high fructose corn syrup, and salt that is contained in packaged foods. Do you really want to put these substances in your body? Most countries insist that genetically modified organisms (GMOs) be listed in the contents on food packaging. The food industry has resisted these listings in the United States. Very often these GMOs use viruses to link molecules to form new organisms. The effect that these viruses have on the human constitution is not clear. However, you the consumer are unaware that you are digesting them.

You may have heard the expression *eat local*, which means to eat foods that are grown and cultivated within a fifty or one hundred mile radius from where you live. This is the best way to insure that you are getting foods that are fresh, not artificially preserved for transport, and that are appropriate for your constitution and the climate where you live. Eating locally produced foods reduces the amount of fossil fuel that would otherwise be used to grow, cultivate, harvest, and transport these foods to your area, while at the same time supporting your local economy. Buying foods that are grown locally enables the farmers in your area to maintain their smaller family farms and enterprises.

Exercise in the outdoors is the best thing you can do for your body to keep it fit. Sunlight is imperative for vitamin D production. Doctors are just beginning to understand the effects that the lack of vitamin D has on our systems. We spend too much time indoors under artificial light and have deprived ourselves of the value of working and playing outdoors. We are beings of light, comprised of electromagnetic molecules. We need the sun to function. There are so many things you can do outside that will help you keep your body in good condition. Ride a bike, take a walk, hike, go swimming, play in the snow, garden, volunteer in a nursing home and push elderly souls around in wheelchairs so they get some sunlight, learn a trade that keeps you outdoors. There are countless things you can do that don't require the cost of a gym membership.

In the last chapter we discussed the value of meditation in the maintenance and healing of the mind and body. There are many forms of exercise that combine the power of meditation with physical movements to improve body functioning. You can get information about yoga practices, tai chi, qigong, and karate online that will further enhance your ability to stay fit and healthy. These disciplines assist in better body, mind, and emotional functioning and help to keep you fit

When you stay healthy and keep your body in good shape, you have a discipline over your mind and body that will add to your happiness. It has been shown that endorphins are released during exercise, which can elevate your mood.

Happiness is something you can generate. There is nothing outside of you that will give you happiness. It is within you to create that essence. It is amazing to think that the US Constitution guarantees "the pursuit of happiness." Most people take that as an inducement to search for that quality outside of themselves. Happiness is what you emanate. The search for happiness takes place within you. The game of life is to find ways to express happiness from within yourself. That can be hard when you are conditioned to see only what is lacking in everything around you, including what is lacking in yourself. Once again, the barrage of ads for products that will make you feel, look, and be better is endless. The message is that you are never enough. The truth is that you are more than enough. Your body is a beautifully designed machine that has all the chemical know-how within each cell to maintain your overall well-being. Your role is to furnish that machine with the essential ingredients that will keep its engines running smoothly.

How do you generate happiness? That is the million dollar question. Happiness is a state of mind. You can generate the thoughts that produce the chemicals that will produce a sense of happiness within yourself. It all comes down to the thoughts you are willing to hold within yourself. You can be happy or you can be sad, depending on how you look at it. What are you seeing within your mind, and what are you hearing yourself say? Those images, those thoughts are what create your emotional reactions. You do have control over them. When you find yourself slumping into a dark hole of bad feelings, go take a walk, play with an animal, do some form of exercise. You can use your body to elevate your mood.

Have you ever been in a bad mood, and then your best friend calls and you are immediately uplifted? You changed your mood in an instant. In that case it was an outside stimulus. What if you used that same ability to shift a mood by changing your thought patterns and taking control of the feelings in your body by stimulating the very chemicals that will bring you to a happier place? That's exactly what exercising, dancing, swimming, and walking can do. Do you think you have that much power or that much control over yourself? Well, you do. As the expression goes: "The proof is in the pudding." Your moods can change on a dime. The trick is to be the director of the moods you want to express, and to take control of how you respond. Try it out for a day and see how you do. When you notice a feeling that gets you down, see if you can shift that feeling to one that elevates you and gives you a sense of well-being or peace. You can generate that peace with some physical activity that puts you in a better frame of mind.

Try This for Yourself

- Keep a journal of what you eat.

- Divide the page into two columns: Healthy and Unhealthy.

- List the foods you eat each day under the appropriate column.

- Start to eliminate foods that you see do not give you the nutrients you need.

- After one week give yourself a reward for becoming more aware of your body.

- Do some form of exercise each day for at least twenty minutes.

- Keep yourself heart healthy. Think and speak from your heart. Your heart is the pump that generates your overall health. Trust your heart. When you feel stressed or ill at ease, check in with your heart. Take a moment to listen to your heart and follow what it asks you to do. Send your breath to your heart to calm it down.

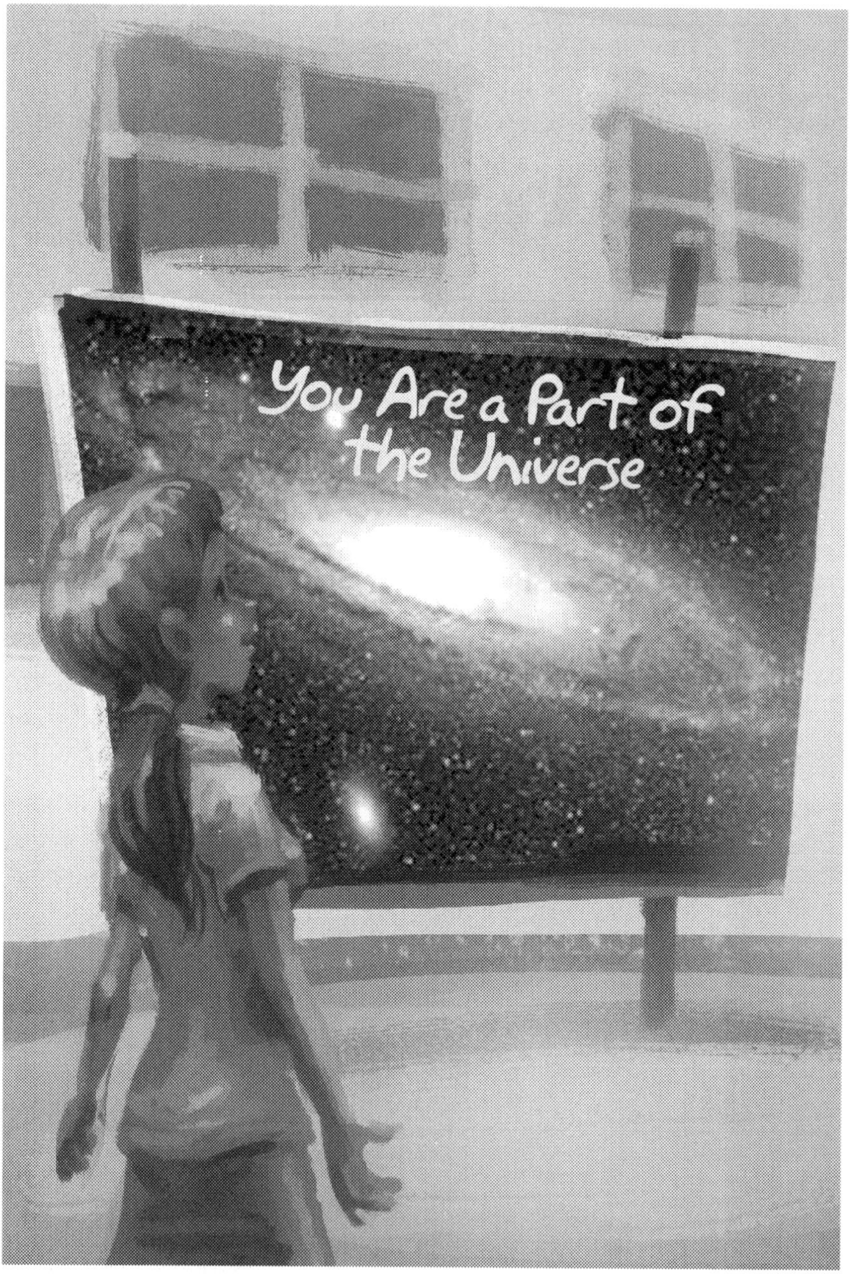
You Are a Part of
the Universe

CHAPTER 5

Expanding My Boundaries
Seeing Myself As a Child of the Universe

What you cannot see in the world is far more
powerful than anything you can see.

—*T. Harv Eker*

In chapter 1 we talked about the electromagnetic molecules that are all around you. You are a part of this web of molecules. It is your substance. As much as all solid matter is nothing but molecules in flux, so too, is your body. In reality there are no boundaries. You are in a constant dance with the molecules that surround you. Nothing is defined, nothing actually touches, we are all part of one big ocean of interacting molecules. We are all swimming in a sea of atoms and particles. We are made of the same substances of stars and planets. We are each unique, and yet we are each made up of the same substances that are inherent in the stars. We are all children of the universe, since we are comprised of its elements. Our interconnection with all that exists is a great mystery. Some recent discoveries in the field of quantum physics are pointing to just that awareness. The secrets of the universe have been the quest of all the great minds from antiquity to the present.

Your gifts, your talents, your uniqueness lie in your ability to be aware, to perceive, to understand your surroundings, and to make sense of what you see and experience. You have the ability to communicate with others about these perceptions. This is a unique gift. You are a part of the universe, and you can understand and appreciate your place in this great mystery. Your role as a child of the universe is to understand your part, and your place within that scheme. How do you fit in? What are your gifts and unique talents? What interests you the most? Where do you find the most satisfaction? Where do you see yourself growing the most and being the most fulfilled? This quest is yours and only yours. Your life is the discovery of the answers to those questions. This period of your life is the time for you to explore all the possibilities that are open to you and to explore your own special development. The cusp between childhood and adulthood is an auspicious time of life.

For many early communal cultures it was a time of great ceremony and celebration. The vision quest was a ceremonial rite of passage used by various Native American tribes to initiate their teenagers in the passage from childhood into adulthood. A teenage boy who had shown readiness would spend several days alone in the wilderness to capture a dream or a vision that would serve as a guiding force to carry him through his life. It was the quester's time to connect to and receive wisdom and insights from the universal forces of nature, the Great Mystery as termed by native cultures.

Seeing who you are and what your place in the universe can be is a daunting matter. It calls for a time of contemplation, soul-searching, and personal inquiry. It is imperative that you give yourself time to dream and to daydream. Your dreams are important and hold many keys to your subconscious mind, which we've not spoken about up to this point. But it is important to point out its function at this stage of your journey to awareness. There are many memories, thoughts, experiences, feelings, reactions, and images that are buried below your conscious awareness. Very often these are buried deep within your psyche, embedded in parts of your brain, and sometimes even in parts of your body in the form of muscle memory. These memories are part of who we are. Bringing their influences to light and discovering the impact they have on you and the value they can offer to your development is an important part of your journey.

Dreams can offer insights into things that are held within the subconscious. The state between waking and sleep can also provide moments of insight and discovery. It is said that Thomas Edison, one of the most prolific American inventors, would not allow himself to fall into a deep sleep. Holding weights in his hand, he would let himself doze off, only to be awakened when the weights fell to the floor. Keeping himself in this constant state between sleep and wakefulness probably allowed him to maintain an almost continual Alpha brain wave state. No wonder he was so creative!

I'm not saying that you should not have a good night's sleep. What is important is to see the value of dreaming as well as daydreaming. Relaxing the mind and allowing thoughts to appear or manifest can be extremely instrumental in the process of discerning what you really want to do with your life. Einstein was a great daydreamer, and we certainly do not underestimate what he achieved.

A favorite amongst many of the students I taught was T.H. Whyte's *The Once and Future King*. The character of Merlin was particularly fascinating because he was living his life backward. He knew the future because he lived it. The students reading this book liked to do an assignment we called the Merlin experiment, in which they would explore their lives at intervals from twenty years into the future, to fifteen years, to ten years, to five, and then one. We would start this as a guided meditation exercise. The students would discuss and then write down what they had seen during the guided fantasy. The meditation script would go something like this:

Close your eyes

Take some time to relax.

Slowly count down from ten to one.

See yourself twenty years from now. It is 20…

What are you wearing?

What are you doing?

How are you employed?

Where are you living?

How are you enjoying yourself?

See yourself fifteen years from now. It is 20…

Ask similar questions.

Do the same for ten, five, and one year into the future.

You can do this exercise on your own or with someone's help. Take some time to write down what you saw at the various time intervals. See if there are some goals you might want to achieve for yourself that become evident by doing this exercise. Then look at what you are doing now to work toward those goals.

Discovering who you are, what you want to be, and how you want to express yourself is no one's business but your own. There is really no one who can tell you what or who you should be or what you should do. It is something you need to determine for yourself. It is also something you need to achieve for yourself. Part of the process of that discovery is seeking out ways to achieve the goals you set for yourself.

Try This for Yourself

Another fun exercise is to create a *vision board* or collage. Creating a vision board is one way to focus on those things you want to have in your future. You will get to create a pictorial representation of the most important and significant things you want to see and have in your life.

You will need a large piece of construction paper, magazines, newspapers, glue and a pair of scissors.

- Go through the magazines and newspapers and tear out any pictures, words or phrases that catch your eye.

- Spend some time arranging those pictures, words and phrases on the large piece of paper until they create a collage of things that want your life to express.

- When you've arrange the pictures, phrases and words on the paper in a way that most appeals to you then glue them on.

- Hang your collage in your room so that you can see what you want to create for yourself.

- Take note of the things in your collage that start to manifest and come into existence.

CHAPTER 6

Walking in Beauty
Honoring Mother Earth

Humankind has not woven the web of life.
We are but one thread within it. Whatever
we do to the web, we do to ourselves.

All things are bound together. All things connect.

—Chief Seattle

According to legend, Black Elk, a Lakota medicine man, was given a message from the White Buffalo Calf Woman during a vision. He was instructed to tell his people to "walk in beauty, for every step you take is sacred." Honoring the earth and all its creatures is an important part of Lakota law, and according to Black Elk, the best way to follow that prescript is to carry oneself through life in a sacred manner. This belief proclaims that everything that surrounds you in your environment is a gift from the Great Mystery and is therefore to be honored.

The Lakota people of the Great Plains saw a reflection of themselves in everything of the earth and in the universe. This is what they call the Great Mystery, our concept of the universe. Whether it be the trees, the rocks, the soil, the animals, the birds, the air we breathe, or the stars that twinkle at night, all these things are composed of the same elements that form us, and so are a part of this Great Mystery. In the world of the Lakota, as with many other Native tribes throughout the Americas, everything has life, even those things that we assume to be inanimate.

In South America, indigenous people call our planet Earth *Pachamama*, or Mother. According to their beliefs, she is very much alive because she is the one who birthed us all. From the earth, we were created, we sprang, and we evolved. If we begin to recognize the earth as our mother, we begin to have a very different relationship with her. The country of Ecuador has included in its constitution the provision that Mother Earth has rights. Ecuador is the first country to recognize and to honor the value of our planet as the entity that provides life and sustenance for us all.

Appreciating our planet and our place on this beautiful blue orb, even as the metaphor of a mother, can help us to understand our relationship and our interconnectedness with all her elements, including the air we breathe, the water we drink, the soil we cultivate, the animals and plants we consume, the minerals we extract for our use, and the fuels we use to power our machines. If we strip the earth of her resources without any concern for the effects on her resilience, we are ultimately destroying our own nurturer.

What if you perceived everything around you as beautiful, or you looked for beauty in your everyday awareness? What if you saw every step that you take as a step into beauty, a step taken with a sense of sacredness? What if you did walk in beauty every day? What if every step you took was sacred? Take some time to see the beauty around you. Start small; you may be surprised. The blue of the sky, a small bird fluttering to find food, the sound of the wind, the wonderful architectural designs on the tops of buildings … Who knows what will capture your attention?

Sometimes the circumstances in your life will cause you to shift your sails to accommodate to the changing winds. I found this to be the case, as I mentioned before, when I was cut from my job at Beach Channel High School during one of the budget crunches in New York City. I was teaching under a speech license and had acquired seniority. However, the Department of Education did away with that license. I was able to get re-certified in English, but unfortunately this caused me to lose my seniority. There was no way that I was going to be able to retain my job. I saw this as an impetus to try new ventures. I wrote to one of my professors at Northwestern to inquire about job leads. She let me know about a position available at the American Conservatory Theatre (ACT) in San Francisco. They were looking for a teacher and a director for their Young Conservatory Theatre program. It seemed an ideal position for me. I would have to go out there for the interview.

I decided to drive to California, taking it as an opportunity to see the country. The interview went very well. On my way back to New York, I stopped at the Grand Canyon, at the Desert View lookout, where there is a replica of a *kiva* (a Hopi ceremonial chamber). I went inside and saw amazing Native American paintings on the walls. Struck by the beauty of these paintings, I began to weep. I had never realized the wisdom, power, and intelligence of Native American life. My major exposure to Native American life up to that point had come from what I saw in TV and films. I went outside the kiva as the sun was setting over the Grand Canyon. Six points came out of the sun. It was an incredibly spectacular sight. I vowed at that time that if I did get the job at ACT, I would produce a show that represented the wisdom that I had perceived in the kiva paintings.

I did get the position at ACT. The theatre was under the direction of Bill Ball, who had directed the production that I had seen when I was sixteen of *Six Characters in Search of an Author* by Luigi Pirandello. I spent the next two years searching for material that would express the sensibilities I had experienced in the kiva. I finally found a story in *The Portable North American Reader*, edited by Frederich W. Turner III. The story that caught my imagination was "The Singing Stone," written by Hyemeyohsts Storm. I brought the story to the director of the Young Conservatory. She told me that the story came from a book called *Seven Arrows*. She had been waiting for someone to dramatize it. She lent me the book, and I read it through that night. I was so moved by the book. The seven arrows are teaching arrows that point the reader in the direction of inner wisdom and connectedness with the earth. It was exactly the material that would allow me to fulfill the vow I had made at Desert View.

The students from the Young Conservatory worked with me in creating this show. We called our production *The Medicine Wheel Way*. We started with the premise that you can see yourself in everything around you because the universe is your reflection. The message is that you are a part of everything you see around you. We wanted to create this experience for the audience, and thought that the use of holograms would give us the ability to show these reflections in a magical way. Unfortunately, the cost of one custom-made hologram at that time was thousands of dollars, which was definitely not within our budget.

I was taking classes at San Francisco State University, where I met a group of fellows who were experimenting with laser light and a technique called *crystal vision*. They had designed custom-made crystals on rotating motors through which they projected slides of images such as starscapes and scenes from nature. The effect was spectacular as the images were refracted around the room. It was exactly what I was hoping to achieve for *The Medicine Wheel Way*. They agreed to assist me with the production.

The last link was to create music for the production. Doug McKecknie, a synthesizer composer, agreed to provide music for the production. The children from the Young Conservatory were the performers.

Seven Arrows is a life-altering book. I highly recommend that you find a copy and read through it, as it is filled with wonderful stories and archival pictures of early Native American life. There are beautiful peace shields designed by Hyemeyohsts Storm and drawn by Karen Harris that help to illustrate the messages in the book's stories. Many of the stories involve animals. We did many exercises that explored the students' relationship to animals: how they moved, how they felt, what frightened them, and how they experienced their environment. The students made masks that represented their animals. They created peace shields of their own that revealed their inner strengths and what they wanted others to know about their talents, gifts, and the contributions they had to offer. Karen Harris's shields from *Seven Arrows* were a great inspiration.

The most wonderful experience was seeing how the young actors brought the stories to life. They understood the material; they understood the message; and they portrayed the essence of the lessons that Hyemeyohsts Storm revealed.

Those who worked on this show had a profoundly transformational experience. The concept of the interconnectedness of all life became a reality for all of us who joined our energies to create this event. I don't think any of us were ever the same afterward. I know my life took on new meaning, and my awareness became more heightened to the wonders, miracles, and beauty all around me. I am very grateful for having had that experience. It has opened me to see the world in a very different way.

Right after the show was performed, I returned to New York for a visit, and on my journey back to California by car, I stopped at a rest stop in a remote part of Nebraska. I thought it odd to find a bookstore inside the rest stop. While I was looking at some maps, an elderly woman behind the counter asked if she could help me. I told her I was interested in the Plains Indians. She pulled open a map and said, "You've already passed the Nebraska tribes, but if you are really interested in the Plains Indians, you'll go out of your way and take Route 2 up to South Dakota. You can go to Mission and the Rosebud reservation. It will be an education in itself. It may be two days out of your way, but it will be worth it."

I got back in my car and headed for Route 2. I kept thinking that this woman must have been a cosmic plant to be in the middle of nowhere to tell me to head up to South Dakota. Having just completed *The Medicine Wheel Way*, I felt the urge to follow the sign I had been given by this woman.

The drive along Route 2 was a very long stretch. It was a clear and sunny day. To keep myself occupied, I took to pulling off the road every time I saw an historical road marker. I learned about early grange meetings and railroad accidents. Just as I was approaching the South Dakota border the sky suddenly changed. There were tiny little clouds that looked like eyes. It reminded me of a dream I once had in which I was scared by eyes looking down at me from above until I had the courage to stare back at them. Then I discovered in the dream it was Thomas Jefferson and Benjamin Franklin looking down on me to offer help. When I saw the clouds over

South Dakota, I realized that the clouds were like the eyes in my dream, only now I could relate to them as the grandfathers in the sky often referred to in Native American stories. I looked at the clouds and declared, "Okay, grandfathers, lead me to what I'm supposed to learn while in this territory."

I drove directly to Mission Reservation. It was about eight o'clock at night. Approaching the entrance, I saw an armed sentry. I had imagined a warmer welcome and directions to a bookstore. I recalled the woman at the rest stop telling me that this journey would be an education in itself. It was not the education I had expected. I quickly turned around and headed west on Route 18. I found a similar experience at the Rosebud Reservation. It was now close to nine o'clock.

I heard on the radio that a severe storm was approaching the area. Given that South Dakota is such a vast place, I did not feel much concern. As I was leaving the area of Rosebud, I looked up and saw a large black cloud above the road. The cloud was shaped like a buffalo. I looked up again and again, and had to confirm that indeed this cloud had the appearance of a buffalo. Not long after that, large lightning bolts started to hit the road all around my car. I was petrified. At times the road would curve away from the lightning, and I would feel relief; then it would curve right back into the midst of the blasts. I decided to stay in the car, protected by my rubber tires. My only fear was that a blast would hit the road in front of my car and pull the pavement apart, causing an accident in that way.

I kept trying to get the radio to work, without much luck. I did hear an announcer say in one brief moment of reception that, "This is a strange storm because there is no thunder." I realized he was right. There was no thunder, only these huge direct bolts hitting the ground.

While driving through this storm, I saw a huge painting of the jumping mouse peace shield on the side of a barn. This was a rendition of one of Karen Harris's shields created for *Seven Arrows*. It must have been two stories high and just as wide. It felt like an apparition, considering it was the shield that represented my favorite story from the book.

The road took me through the Wounded Knee area. As the road curved past Wounded Knee, I drove under an archway of purple lightning, after which the storm subsided. I had traveled almost the entire width of South Dakota. I followed the road up into the hills. It was now around eleven o'clock at night. I could smell the sulfur in the air from the aftermath of the lightning. The air was clearing. I looked up and saw the same cloud I had seen at the beginning of the storm back at Rosebud. It was now white and appeared to be a white buffalo. I looked again and again to confirm that it was indeed a cloud of the same shape as I had seen before. In Black Elk's legend he describes his experience with the White Buffalo Calf Woman. When she is about to leave, she turns to him and has the head of a black buffalo and then walks away only to turn back again, now with the head of a white buffalo. I pulled into an overlook high up on a cliff above the great plains below. I could see the storm still raging in the distance as I experienced a calm summer night around me.

The next day I was driving through Nevada. I had the map that the woman in Nebraska had given me. I looked at the map and saw Pyramid Lake Indian reservation. I thought that since it was daytime I might be more readily able to enter, and maybe then I would find a bookstore. My own cultural biases ran deep. I was cut short along the route I had taken by a barbed wire fence that proclaimed Government Testing: Do Not Enter. I pulled out the map once again to look more carefully and noticed how many testing sites were in and around what was designated as Indian territory. I figured another route to take to Pyramid Lake.

Upon entering the approach to Pyramid Lake you travel through a red desert. The energy is antediluvian. You might expect to see a dinosaur coming up over one of the hills. I noticed an historic marker on the side of the road, and as was my habit, I pulled over to read it. It stated that young Chief Winnamucca, a superior man of any race, had successfully warded off the American cavalry on two different occasions with only one hundred of his fellow warriors. This area is a Paiute reservation, and all hunting and fishing licenses had to be obtained through the tribe. It was clear from the energy of this place that the land belonged to the Paiutes. There was something magical about it.

The lake is named for the natural pyramid that stands in its middle. The road into Pyramid Lake is like a journey back in time. On the day that I was there the sky was very blue, and circling around the tips of the pyramid were several lenticular clouds that looked like space ships. It was a magnificent sight. On the road leaving the reservation I spied another historic marker. It stated that Pyramid Lake is the remains of Lake Bonneville, which had been an ice age lake. The largest trout in the world are found there because of all the calcium deposits that empty into the lake.

What was the significance of these two experiences? What was the education that I received from visiting these two places? I later read in *Bury My Heart at Wounded Knee* by Dee Brown that it was a Paiute named Wovoka who taught the ghost dance to two Lakota braves. The ghost dance was thought to magically protect the wearer from cavalry bullets. The two braves returned to Wounded Knee camp to teach the ghost dance to the people living there. The Cheyenne and Sioux who were camped at Wounded Knee started to practice the ghost dance. The US became suspicious of this and felt that those who had settled at Wounded Knee were planning some sort of uprising. It was this suspicion that prompted the attack on what were primarily women, children, and the elderly camped at Wounded Knee.

Years later, I was in South Dakota and was advised to visit the site where Black Elk had his vision. Black Elk, the noted Lakota medicine man, had witnessed the massacre at Wounded Knee. He saw the threat of Western culture to Native American wisdom and traditions. He held the vision that his tribe members were given the responsibility to be caretakers of the earth and to preserve the sacredness of the *red road*, the path of beauty that each Native American was born to travel.

Although it was early October, there had been a blizzard that dropped two feet of snow. By the time I set out the following day it was warm and most of the snow had already melted. Having come from New York City, I was not prepared for snow, never mind a blizzard. When I arrived at the trailhead that led to the place where Black Elk had purportedly experienced his vision, I was stopped by all the snow remaining in these hills. Some hikers were coming down the trail and they suggested that I walk in their tracks. This was a good suggestion; it helped me start the climb. As I continued, the trail became more difficult and I was tempted to give up. I thought I had come this far and no one would know or care if I ever made it all the way up to the top. I sat down on a large rock and contemplated my descent when two birds started to chirp wildly on a tree in front of me. I ignored them at first, but they kept flying upward and then back down to the tree I sat in front of and chirped louder and louder. I took it as a sign to go on and not give up. The snow was getting higher; my shoes were getting wetter; and the ascent was getting more difficult. I was by myself, and again I thought it foolish to continue. Again I sat on a fallen log and thought about a retreat. Once again, the birds returned and chirped more and more frantically, moving farther up the hill and back to where I sat. I realized they were not going to give up on me, so I continued.

When I came to the next level, there was an outcrop, and before me I could see for miles and miles naturally formed limestone spires that looked like cathedral spires extending into the distance. It was one of the most glorious sights I have ever seen. This created the most glorious natural cathedral you could imagine. The birds flew around me and then left. I am so glad that I trusted the birds.

There is a different sort of energy that you can experience when you start to open to the understanding that there are miracles and magic in everything that surrounds you. It is time for us in the modern world to open to the insights and understandings of those indigenous people who have traditions that honor the earth, through our own direct experience of nature and the world around us. It's all in your perception and perspective—in the way you see the things around you.

Try This for Yourself—The Sense Walk

- Find a place outside to sit quietly with your eyes closed.

- Listen for the sounds around you.

- Distinguish man-made sounds from natural sounds.

- Get up and start to walk slowly in a meandering path.

- Walk for a while looking down.

- Walk for a while looking up.

- Walk briskly for a while, then end it in a run.

- Stop at an intersection and watch the dance of people and traffic.

- Look at the structure of buildings and notice any interesting architectural designs on the tops.

- Take a moment to feel the texture of the materials used for one of these buildings.

- Find a tree and feel its texture.

- Sit quietly again and notice how you feel.

A Native American Prayer

O Great Spirit,

Whose voice I hear in the winds, and whose breath gives life, life to all the world, hear me!

I am small and weak. I need your strength and wisdom.

Let me walk in beauty, and make my eyes ever behold the red and purple sunset.

Make my hands respect the things you have made and my ears sharp to hear your voice.

Make me wise so that I may understand the things you have taught my people.

Let me learn the lessons you have hidden in every rock and leaf.

I seek strength, not to be greater than my brother, but to fight my greatest enemy, which is myself.

Make me always ready to come to you with clean hands and straight eyes.

So when life fades as the falling sunset, my spirit may come to you without shame.

—Author Unknown

CHAPTER 7

Things Fall Apart
Now What?

> *When I defend myself, I am attacked.*
>
> —*The Course in Miracles, lesson 135*

No journey on the road to awareness would be complete without a truthful discussion of the pitfalls that might beset you and distract you from staying on your personal quest. This may be hard to say, and even harder still to accept, but things do have a tendency to fall apart.

While teaching a ninth grade class at Edward R. Murrow in Brooklyn, I was given the assignment to teach the book *Things Fall Apart* by Chinua Achebe. This was a very bright group of students. They were smart, they were talented, they were good-spirited, and they had the whole world ahead of them. I was disturbed that I had to introduce them to this book. I thought that if they merely kept a positive attitude, their lives would be wonderful and successful, and they would achieve everything their hearts desired. The book ends with the downfall of the main character because his world really does fall apart. Why should I bring such a gloom and doom awareness into their lives at such an early age?

The main character in *Things Fall Apart* is Okonkwo, a self-righteous man who prides himself on his standing in his traditional African community. He is not willing, nor is he equipped to allow for the changes that were

51

introduced by the invading white culture. His resistance to change brings his downfall. Trying desperately to hold onto his own value system causes him to make decisions that are not in step with the changing times.

This is a great lesson for us, too. Attempting to hold on to your own outmoded patterns or ways of acting or behaving may be a hindrance to seeing a better or more productive path.

I now apologize for my naiveté in being reluctant to introduce *Things Fall Apart* to my students. I realize that resilience is probably one of the most important traits you can acquire. It is a reality that things will fall apart in your life. Not everything is going to work out according to plan. There may be setbacks, but the spirit to continue, the energy to carry on, the good will to trust in the best, and to keep a happy attitude no matter what befalls you might be the most important ability you can develop. Change will happen. Change is the only constant according to Buddhist teachings. Sometimes things will go in your favor and sometimes they will not. How you respond to the different experiences, whether good or bad, is the key to your success. I am sure you have heard of the thousand attempts Thomas Edison made when inventing the light bulb until he lit upon the one that finally worked. He did not let failure stop him. Failure will happen, things will not work out the way you want, and there are times when it appears that nothing will ever go right again. However, therein lies the opportunity to carry on despite setbacks.

You can choose the direction you take in any situation that comes your way in life. How you choose and what you choose is up to you.

Saul Bruckner, the first principal at Edward R. Murrow, was an inspiration to both the students and staff. He believed that the more you give students freedom, the more they will choose to be responsible. He made clear that our job as teachers was to provide our students enticing learning experiences to keep them engaged. He often said that our job as teachers was not to give the students information, but to enhance their ability to choose directions for themselves.

Choosing a course of action, choosing the best areas to pursue in life, choosing the right friends, choosing how you spend your time, and what you put into your body are all part of the process of developing an awareness of the power you have over your own destiny. There are no right answers and there are no surefire prescriptions for how to do life right. The ultimate decisions are yours. It is up to each individual to make those choices.

It is also important to know when to hold steady when life throws you blows, also to know when to change direction, when it is clear that you have made some mistakes. Life will not always unfold the way you would like. If anything, the way life unfolds will be unpredictable. You can't hold onto your expectations of how things ought to be according to you own designs. Success comes from accepting the inevitable and dancing with all the possibilities that may arise.

Things will change. Life has a tendency toward entropy, which Merriam-Webster describes as "a process of degradation or running down or a trend to disorder." These changes will occur more quickly than any of us can imagine. Technology will change; the climate will continue to spiral out of control; governments will rise and fall; and the world's financial markets will continue to be in flux. The ability to accept these changes and challenges, and to be aware of what will be necessary to do next will be the order of the day. The key word is *resilience*, the "ability to recover from or adjust easily to misfortune or change," again according to Merriam-Webster.

I don't know what has become of those wonderful students who were in that ninth grade class at Edward R. Murrow. I do know that my own life has been a series of wins and losses. I have had to roll with the punches and adjust my course because of unforeseeable obstacles that occurred in my path. One thing I know for sure is that with each change came incredible growth, the potential to discover new ways of thinking, and the opportunity to meet new and wonderful people along the way.

I loved teaching at Beach Channel in Rockaway; however, when New York City had a terrible financial crunch, there were severe layoffs in the Department of Education. My speech license was dissolved, and I found myself without a job. It was that situation that led me to the American Conservatory Theatre in San Francisco. I never would have been involved with a large regional theatre company if my fortunes had not been reversed and I had not lost my license.

Try This for Yourself

- When things do fall apart, be honest about your losses.

- Make a list of all you are losing.

- Then tear it up and throw it away. Those losses are gone. You have no need to hold onto them anymore.

- Avoid dwelling on the past losses.

- Now make a list of what you want to achieve and put that up on your mirror or refrigerator.

- Reflect on that for a while and then add to that list what you need to do to achieve those things.

- Keep your focus on what is next, what lies ahead. Keep your eyes open and looking forward.

Some people have to face horrifying situations such as a diagnosis of a terminal disease, or losing one's home and possessions in a devastating flood. Why is it that some people never recover from such horrific experiences, while others find determination, opportunities, and even joy from such conditions? It is all in the way you regard the story. What story are you going to tell about the way life treats you? Are you going to be the victor or the victim? What story are you going to tell about your ability to overcome disaster, misfortune, setbacks, and loss? It is all up to your interpretation. We don't have control over the circumstance that life throws at us, but we do have control over the way we respond. Our response is based on our interpretation. It correlates to the way we see the situation. Will you see an opportunity or a disaster?

Nelson Mandela is another African man who can provide a great lesson for maintaining one's commitment to a desired goal no matter what circumstances arise, no matter what challenges appear to disrupt your progress, and no matter how much your world may be falling apart. He was committed to peace and unity for all people in South Africa. There were many who opposed him, and there were powerful forces working against him. Despite the threats, violence, and attempts to undermine his cause, he held firm to his vision to unite all of South Africa, both blacks and whites, in a unifying government. He was incarcerated for twenty-seven years, initially on Robben Island, but he never gave up his will or determination. He was eventually released from prison and was able to transform an entire nation. He was elected the first black president of South Africa. He did not see any value in anger, hate, violence, or revenge in bringing South Africa into a new era of racial unity. His legacy will be remembered and revered by the international community.

No matter what your age, no matter what your circumstances, no matter where you may find yourself or what position you may be in, you will always be given opportunities to make a difference, settle a dispute, or save a situation from disaster. You can take a moment to transform the energy within you from scared to sacred and use that energy to see you through misfortunes.

One of the students from Beach Channel was a wonderful Hispanic boy who lived in Spanish Harlem. He traveled three hours every day by train to get to Beach Channel by 8 a.m. Every summer many of the students who were studying oceanography at this magnet school got the opportunity to join the Coast Guard on treks to different parts of the world. In early June you would hear announcements on the school's PA system inviting students to meet with Coast Guard representatives to discuss trips to the Amazon, Nova Scotia, or Greenland. This particular boy was selected to go on a trip to Greenland. While out at sea, the Coast Guard ship intercepted a Russian fishing boat within the border designated for no commercial fishing. It became an international incident. Unfortunately, no one on the American ship could speak Russian and no one on the Russian boat spoke English. The young man from Beach Channel spoke Spanish, and fortunately there was one Russian sailor who spoke Spanish as well.

The article in *The New York Times* describing this event stated that this fifteen-year-old boy settled an international incident with his diplomacy and good will. In this case, good will saved the day and helped avoid what might have been an unfortunate outcome. It takes courage to promote good will in all situations, and in the example given a fifteen-year-old was capable of that distinction.

There will be unsettling incidents in your life. There will be circumstances that will knock you for a loop. There will be some people who will want to do you harm. The way you maintain your resolve, the manner in which you stay true to your values, and the dignity with which you maintain yourself will be the determining factors in your ability to weather any storm and to succeed in what truly matters to you.

You may like to try this exercise when you experience those rocky times and bumps along your path. It is a guided meditation that you may like to try on your own or have someone guide you through.

The Rescue Mission

- Sit comfortably and relax by counting down from ten to one.

- Imagine that you are on a raft in the middle of the ocean and the waves are gently rocking you along in the water.

- Imagine that your raft slowly starts to move toward the shore of a beautiful island. Let the raft gently come up onto the beach.

- Step off the raft and look around. You see a path leading to a beautiful garden and you follow the path.

- Sit down in the garden and take a few deep breaths. You can smell the flowers and hear the birds sing.

- Look around and notice something that is in the garden for you. It is a powerful object that has been put there to help you. Pick up the object.

- It is now time to continue. You start to walk up a mountainous slope.

- When you arrive at the top of this slope, you see the situation or the person that has been troubling you.

- See if the object you found in the garden can help you.

- An animal now appears that is there to help you with this situation. Observe how the animal helps to rescue you and resolves the issue.

- When all has been resolved to your satisfaction, bid the animal farewell.

- When you feel strong and complete, notice that an object has been left on the ground for you. It is something for you to take back to keep you safe.

- Walk back down the incline through the garden and back to the beach.

- Get back on the raft and allow the current to take you out to sea again.

- Breathe deeply. You are now safe.

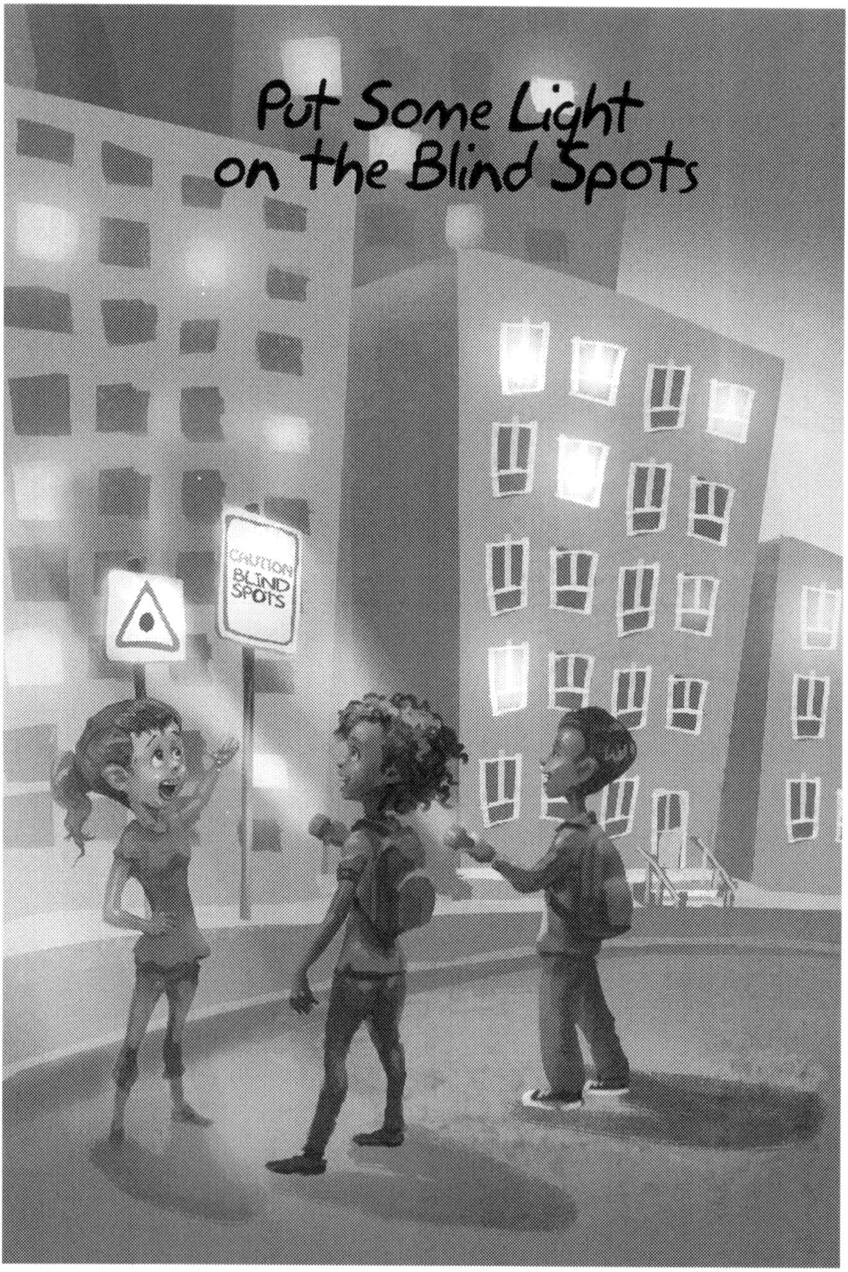
Put Some Light on the Blind Spots
CAUTION
BLIND SPOTS

CHAPTER 8

Putting Some Light on the Shadow
Dealing with the Dark Side

Life is like photography; you need the negatives to develop.

—Unknown

In the last chapter we discussed the reversal of fortune that can come when situations beyond your control dictate a change of direction that might be necessary for you to take in your life. We looked at ways you can arm yourself in the face of sudden and difficult challenges. We also saw the value of being in control of the way you interpret the circumstances of each situation that you face in order to better understand the value of every lesson on the road to awareness.

There is another factor to consider. It is also important to look at the way in which you may become your own worst enemy. It may not be an unforeseeable situation that knocks you off course. It may be *you!* There are times when the only saboteur who can deter you from your path is yourself.

This part of our discussion leads us to look at the dark side or the shadow of the personality. Coming to grips with the shadow side of ourselves is one of the most challenging aspects of any individual's life. The *shadow* is a term that refers to the dark side of an individual's personality that is not readily in view. It may be an aspect of ourselves that we would like to hide from others, or it may be a part of ourselves that we are not fully conscious of.

Maybe you are mean at times; maybe you cheat; maybe you hide things from others or talk behind their backs; or maybe you let your anger get the best of you. Any behavior that undermines your relationships, opportunities, success, or progress can be part of the shadow, the darker part of your personality.

These tendencies could be attributed to experiences you had when you were younger; something someone close to you said; or experiences you had as you are going through life. The reactions you had to any of these can be buried within your subconscious, that part of yourself that is below conscious awareness. The shadow side can manifest itself in moments when we feel threatened, vulnerable, exposed, or frightened. Sometimes we are not even sure why we react the way we do. It may be because the shadow has such a strong grip on our behavior that we are compelled to say or do something we later regret.

You may or may not be aware of these traits. You may have an ability to harness this energy, or you may be at the mercy of these darker behaviors. Everyone is faced with the challenge of integrating their darker forces with more positive ways of behaving. You are not alone. The more you share your journey with others and face your demons, the stronger you will become. You can make friends with the darker elements of yourself by labeling them. "There goes Angry Barbara again," or "Jealous Jack has just shown up." Each of these personality traits tells you something about yourself. It is vital information that enables you to see all sides of yourself.

Looking at the darker sides of yourself calls for soul-searching, honesty, and the ability to admit, when things are not working out the way you would like, that you may be thwarting your own progress. Don't point fingers at anyone else. This calls for pointing the finger at your own heart to see where the trouble may truly reside. It takes strength to admit your own faults, or that you may be the cause of a bad situation. Nobody wants to admit that they are wrong. Most of us are much more interested in proving how right we are. It doesn't take much to see that this one characteristic is at the root of many of our human interactions, struggles, and even wars. "My side is right and your side is wrong, and there is no line I am willing to cross unless you admit that you are at fault."

This kind of thinking is not productive and doesn't allow for much movement or growth. In fact, it's closer to trench warfare, where everyone becomes positional, interested more in their own positions than in hearing another perspective or point of view, and opening up to ways in which everyone flourishes or wins. Allowing for all points of view to be expressed provides for new solutions to emerge.

It takes one brave soul to say maybe I am wrong; maybe I made a mistake; maybe I did some harm; maybe I need to make amends. This seems to be a very difficult thing for most people to do. We would rather stay locked in conflict and spend time mired in unresolved issues. According to Carl Jung, a leading psychological thinker, we all have a dark side, we all have *shadow* aspects of our personality that we would rather not let others see. We are all selfish, greedy, hateful, angry, intolerant, lazy, neglectful. The problem is we often don't like to acknowledge these vices. Thus those aspects of ourselves stay in the shadows. When these elements of our personality stay hidden, we put a lot of energy into covering up our weaknesses. Real power comes from admitting your foibles and bringing them into the light where you can gain insight by acknowledging and accepting all parts of your humanity. When you accept the shadow sides of your personality, you embrace your humanity and you deepen your compassion for yourself and others, because you begin to see how much alike we all are. This acceptance brings you one step ahead on the road to awareness.

An interesting balancing act is going on within you. You are always being challenged to balance the light and dark forces within yourself. It really is a little like *Star Wars*. You remember Luke being told to trust the Force. You can harness the energies within you in the direction you want to take in life. We talked about that in chapter 1. When you are in the flow of positive energy you can experience yourself vibrating at a more harmonious frequency helping you maintain a more harmonious flow. All of creation vibrates with energy, you want to be a clear channel so that you can be in tune with those vibrations. It is a matter of keeping yourself emotionally fit, mentally fit, and physically fit. Thoughts that produce feelings of anxiety, anguish, worry, or anger drain your immune system and damage the function of your cells and deplete your energy. We looked at this is chapter 3. Another way to view this is to understand that negative emotions create static in the electrical signals you are emitting. The energy you give off places you in a field where you will attract to yourself that which is vibrating on your level. If you are projecting a lot of negative energy, then lo and behold, that is what will be drawn to you. In order to keep yourself in harmony with your surroundings, be aware of the energy you are projecting. Your world will very often become a mirror for the energy field you create within and around yourself.

You are *at cause* for whatever happens in your life that results from the ways you react to that which befalls you. It may be hard to accept that reality, because it is easier to pass the blame for our failures on parents, teachers, friends, associates, the government you name it. When you become 100 percent responsible for everything that befalls you, then true mastery can occur. Good, bad, indifferent and so-so occurrences are more easily managed when you take 100 percent responsibility for how any situation will turn out. You are now entering the mastery stage. This takes guts. No grudges, no pointing fingers, no regrets, no feeling sorry for yourself, no blaming others, will allow you to achieve success on the road to awareness. If you want your light to shine in full vibrancy, then you are being challenged to keep your vibrational energy high.

Let's look at the role forgiveness plays in this process. As we saw in the last chapter, there will be times when people do what seems to be bad things to you. You feel betrayed, angry, hurt, resentful, threatened, and defensive. The real or imagined attacks you experience cause you to become untrusting, fearful, withholding, anxious, armored, and closed. You have to live with all of that. Those emotions, those feelings, those ways of being only damage you. You have no control over how people behave. Everyone is accountable for his or her own actions, and everyone will have to pay the price and suffer the consequences for everything they do.

What you can control is the effect that the actions of others have on you. This is where *forgiveness* comes into play. Forgiveness is an internal act. It is the opportunity for you to restore your own equilibrium, your own balance. The act of forgiveness enables you to be able to give again.

Forgiveness is for giving. Your ability to give of yourself, to give to the world, or to give to others will be impeded if you hold onto any of the feelings, emotions, or ways of being described above such as anger, hurt, betrayal, or resentment. You will not be free to experience your own joy, your own love, and your own sense of wonder of the world as long as you are mired in a grudge against someone else. They did what they did. They are accountable for what they did with themselves, with their Creator, and in some cases, with the legal system. Holding a grudge only keeps you tied to them and binds you to these past transgressions. The act of forgiveness is for you, not anyone else. It is not your job to exonerate or provide amnesty for those who harmed you in any way. What is powerful is to trust in the path of awareness that all things in life play out in good time. Trust in your ability to grow, and let your heart open to the wisdom that is at the core of the universe. Shakespeare said, "All the world's a stage and men and women merely players." Life can appear to be one big soap opera. You can detach from the negative drama, and know that everything that is unfolding is a part of a great masterful scheme. Your job is to observe and enjoy what time is given to you. You can become the playwright or director and scope out a magnificent story for yourself.

When I was teaching at Beach Channel High School, the drama club decided to produce the musical *Godspell* by Stephen Schwartz. The principal of this New York City public school was concerned that it might be too religious a play to present at the school. We agreed that we would take out the religious references and concentrate on the parables and stories and the universal lessons contained within them. Some of the students in the play were enrolled in an English class called the Bible as Literature and were really well-versed in their Bible stories. When the principal attended the dress rehearsal he was aghast that there was a crucifixion scene in the play. He demanded that it be cut. He also wanted the song "Long Live God" excluded. The students tried to argue that the crucifixion was an act of history, but their arguments went unheard. This was the afternoon before the opening of the play, so a solution had to be discovered quickly that would not disrupt the production.

The students themselves found a loving and forgiving way to handle what could have been an unfortunate circumstance. Instead of a crucifixion, they had the characters of the play hold back the young man playing Jesus. The analogy that they wanted to convey was that a crucifixion can come in the form of negative forces preventing a person from moving forward or expressing who they are. Instead of "Long Live God," they sang "Long Live Love." For them, God is love, and they sang that song from the bottom of their hearts. I don't think I was ever so moved by a theatrical performance.

Love and forgiveness are powerful forces. They are forces that work for you. They are forces that you can harness to maintain your stride on the road to awareness. These are forces that keep you in balance and help you maintain your harmony with all that is perfect in this world. Moments of being sidetracked by negative energy or dark forces within or outside of yourself will occur on the road to awareness. The more you are able to use these situations as opportunities to reflect on your own inner strength, power, and light, the more you will illuminate the masterful lessons that you can discover along your own route.

It is so easy to throw in the towel and give up. However, this attitude will not keep you on the road to awareness. You may want to give up, call it quits, and not go on. Maintain your resolve and keep going. Trust the signs, stay in tune, keep yourself in harmony. The universe has so many wonderful sights to share with you. Keep your eyes open and keep looking forward.

Try This for Yourself

- Keep a journal and start identifying your shadow personality traits.

- Draw pictures of your shadow personality traits.

- Name them.

- Dialogue with your shadow personalities and see what they have to tell you.

- Do some dream work. Before you go to sleep ask to have a dream about your shadow personality.

- See if your shadow side has anything to say or give you.

- Write these dreams down in your journal.

The following guided imagery can also be of some assistance when letting go of people you want to let go of.

- Count down from ten to one. Keep taking deep breaths as you do and feel yourself going deeper and deeper into a relaxed state.

- Imagine that you are on a dock and that there is a small boat in front of you that is tied to a post.

- Place the person or people on that boat that you want to let go. Imagine that there is a slight mist on the water.

- Untie the rope and let the boat drift off into the water.

- Slowly lose sight of the boat as it disappears into the mist.

Do this exercise as many times as it takes until you feel free of the person who causes you distress.

CHAPTER 9

Finding the Power of My Voice

Who Am I As a Communicator?

I am thankful for all those who said no to me.

It is because of them I'm doing it myself.

—Albert Einstein

Every time you speak you set in motion sound waves that vibrate at a particular *frequency*. These sound waves hit the hammer and anvil in someone's ear and become messages that are sent to that person's brain. The words you choose, your tone level, your inflectional pattern, and your volume all play a part in the frequency you transmit. Others react to your words, as well as to all the other elements that are associated with the sounds you make. Be aware that when you speak you are entering into another person. You can think of this process as a gift or an intrusion depending on the frequency you want to transmit. The same is true in reverse. You may find yourself reacting positively or negatively to something someone says to you because the frequency that you experience may either soothe or jar you. Someone saying a simple thing such as "Come here" can have a totally different effect on you, depending on the tone.

Your voice is a gift. Your voice, whether in the words you speak or the words you write, is your power. Your words represent who you are, what you believe, and what you hold true. You will be judged by your words, by what you say, and how you say it. Who you are will be determined by the way you express yourself. If your words are harsh, demeaning, or hurtful, others may respond in a similar way. If you are soft, gentle, and kind then others can vibrate to that frequency and respond accordingly. It can become a bit of a dance. Once you are on the road to awareness, you will want to determine who you are as a communicator, and how your communications are being interpreted. You will find this true in many venues that you choose to use for communication, whether you are expressing yourself online, on Facebook, or Twitter. The responses you receive will very often match the energy or tone you transmit. You are always communicating. You communicate through your voice, your body, your words, and even through your silence. You can also communicate through various forms of expression, whether through the arts, athletics, science, or academics. You are never not communicating. It is your prerogative to choose your own forms of communication and what exactly you want to say through those forms.

The way you communicate can also change, depending on who you are communicating with and the role you are playing at the time. How you communicate to your younger siblings is probably not the same way you converse with your teachers. You may even change the quality of your communications with your various friends.

Try This for Yourself

This is a role-playing game that you can play with your friends or with your teachers at school.

- Brainstorm all the roles you play in a day, such as child, student, babysitter, mediator, psychologist, friend, enemy, daughter, sister, brother, crybaby, fool, jokester, and the like.

- Write each role on a small sheet of paper and put them into a hat or basket.

- Have each one in the group select a slip of paper with one of the roles written on it.

- Think about how you might play that role in life.

- Create a scene with two or three of your friends in which there is a communication breakdown because of the way these roles interact.

- After each scene is performed, discuss ways in which communication could have been improved in each group.

It is really a fun exercise.

We played this role game at Beach Channel as part of the Interpersonal Communication course that was offered there. In this course the students looked at ways they communicate. They explored their communications as individuals, in one-on-one settings, in small groups, and before large audiences. This role-playing game gave the students a chance to see that they did play many roles in life, and that their behavior could change under different circumstances. They could also see that they did not have to be tied to any one role.

I always encouraged my students to speak up for themselves. When I was teaching at Beach Channel we were working on the production of *Fiddler on the Roof*. The young girl who was playing the Yenta was perfect for the part. Unfortunately, she had to drop out because of family reasons. Another girl in the show wanted to play the part, but she didn't fit my idea of the character. She was tall, she was beautiful, and she was Puerto Rican. She confronted me about my bias, and I was very impressed by her guts, her strength, and to be honest, by her wisdom. I relented and agreed to let her play the part. She was wonderful in the play, and I had to admit I was wrong in my assessment. That young lady went on to perform on Broadway, in the movies, and on TV. She had a voice and she used it to express herself.

Your voice is powerful. You may not always feel that is the case, but it is true. I remember telling my students, "There are only one hundred or so teachers in our school, and there are more than 2,800 of you. You really do have the power. A teacher is hired to serve the students. You have a right to let us know what you need."

More and more schools are becoming so departmentalized that it is hard to find the core, the center, the raison d'être, the reason for existence, of why the students are really there. It may sound funny to you, but most school systems are based on an antiquated system of education that is modeled after the factory system. It is the idea of top down management. There is someone at the top directing middle mangers to get the best work out of the line supervisors who keep the workers in check. Similarly, in education there is the principal who directs the administrators who manage the teachers to keep the students in line. The idea of early public education was to direct students to take their place in the economy in factory model jobs.

Still following this model, education today lacks a holistic approach to learning. You cannot departmentalize subjects any more than you can departmentalize human beings. Not all people learn in the same way, and not all subjects are relevant to all individuals. If you are to find your voice and your place on the planet, you will need to explore the world around you with your own senses, discovering your own voice and your own methodology for expression.

We discussed how many cultures around the world mark the transition from childhood to adulthood by ceremonies, celebrations, or in some cases, by religious rites. It is a momentous time in a human's life. Your chemistry is changing, your hormones are changing, your mind is expanding, and your perceptions are becoming more astute. This is a human's rite of passage. In many societies it is considered the privilege of the community to usher the young person into their new role as a contributing member of that society. This is done in different ways by different cultures. For those of the Jewish religion a bat mitzvah or bar mitzvah is performed. For Christians, a young person may be confirmed. Native Americans may send their young adult on a vision quest, and in the Latin and South American countries a young girl celebrates her fifteenth birthday at a *quinceañera*. In a feudal society a young knight would prove himself by going on a quest. Whatever the form, the underlying motivation was similar: to give a young person an opportunity to find his own voice, his own power, and to take his or her place in the adult world.

Young teens are in an expansive time of life. Historically, people of this age would apprentice with artisans to be trained in specific skills because it is an ideal time to learn and grow. It is a time when you are able to absorb so much information and a great time for you to experiment and choose those things that most delight your fancy. It is time to see many directions and to explore the paths you may want to travel in your life. It is a time when you can allow yourself to be inspired. Determining your voice and your path is your birthright.

While I was teaching at Beach Channel, a group of teachers from across different curriculum areas participated in the Columbia Writers Project. The purpose of the program was to offer writing projects to teachers from various disciplines. The teachers would then give their students opportunities to express themselves in writing experiences, whether in math, science, art, English, and even physical education.

One assignment we all completed was called the "I Quest." I found this writing experience so beneficial that I expanded the idea for my own classes. By the time I was teaching at Jacqueline Kennedy Onassis, the project had evolved into an entire semester event.

Try This Project

The I Quest project worked very well with ninth grade English students who were reading *Once and Future King* by T.H. White. It also worked well to do the Merlin exercise described in chapter 5 as a preliminary to this project. This way students had an idea of where they wanted to see themselves in the future, what was important to them, and what they wanted to achieve for themselves.

- Choose a subject you really want to explore—something where you want to be an expert; something you want to achieve; something you want to master; or something you would like to have happen for yourself, your family, your community, or maybe even for the world.

- Do some research about your topic. Read a book on that topic and three magazine articles related to your area of interest.

- Interview an expert in this area. Develop twenty questions you would like to ask this expert. Set up the interview in person, on the phone, or through the Internet.

- Determine what you want to achieve by becoming an expert in this area.

- Write a three-to-five-page paper describing your discoveries.

- Prepare a three-minute presentation describing your quest, your research, the interview, your accomplishments, and your failures.

- Create a coat of arms that represents a banner, standard, or logo for your quest.

After the presentations we would have a ceremony knighting all those who participated, made a valiant effort, and fulfilled their quests.

Students who participated in these quests became very strong in their ability to choose a path for themselves. They proved to themselves that they could pursue their own course in life. You might say that the project encouraged them to take the first steps for themselves on the road to awareness.

Learning about yourself as a communicator is learning to determine who you are as a communicator, how you relate to others in one-on-one situations, how you relate in a group, and how you can command a larger audience when needed. There may be times when you will be asked to speak in front of a group. There are studies that show that many people are almost as afraid to speak in front of a group as they are afraid of death. When asked to speak in public you may feel your heart racing, sweaty palms, tongue tied, nervous, jittery, and scared. All those symptoms are normal. When you are asked to speak in front of others, your body assists you by supplying you with extra energy. What you are experience is an adrenaline rush. You are being given more energy to be able to command a demanding situation. The idea is to use that energy by giving it away. Holding it back by trying to hide these symptoms doesn't give you the ability to release that energy and use that added strength to send that power out to the crowd. You are being assisted to be more powerful. Expressing that energy is the key.

Use your voice wisely; speak your truth; be aware of your energy and the frequency you are vibrating at. Use your power to communicate to assist your advancement on the road to awareness.

CHAPTER 10

Compassion Is the Fashion

Between stimulus and response there is a space.

*In that space lies our freedom and
power to choose our response.*

In our response lies our growth and freedom.

—Viktor Frankl

Compassion is one of the words most looked up in dictionaries. It is a word whose meaning eludes many. The meaning of compassion can be hard to understand and sometimes even harder to implement. Compassion is "a sympathetic consciousness of others' distress with a desire to alleviate it," says Merriam-Webster. It is a quality that many strive to attain, but have a hard time incorporating into their daily lives. Why is the idea of compassion so elusive and yet so important to comprehend?

Being compassionate starts with compassion for yourself. It starts with being gentle with yourself, accepting your mistakes and weaknesses, and laughing at those times when you are foolish. Compassion also includes extending that same gentleness, acceptance, and understanding to others who may be in the same boat.

Compassion is not a quality that demands some ascetic sage rising above the level of humanity to dole out sympathy to those below. Compassion is experienced by those who accept that all passions are within themselves, and who embrace those passions, whether negative or positive, as a part of their humanity and the humanity of all people on the planet. When you see and accept all parts of yourself as your humanity, you begin to understand and accept the humanity of all those who inhabit the planet with you. Seeing that all passions are within you, you see all passions existing in others as well. This opens the door for compassion.

You may be hurt, and sometimes it takes a long time for the pain to go away. Having feelings that cause you personal suffering, pain, anguish, torment, and remorse is part of the human condition. Coming to see that everyone else on the planet experiences those very same feelings in varying degrees, at various stages in their lives, is the beginning of compassion.

What's the value of having compassion for others? It may seem contrary to what you have been led to believe as the acceptable way to progress in your life. Likely you have been encouraged to look out for yourself, see how you can get ahead, determine what you want to achieve, or figure out how can you measure your success. Many of our school systems are based on a foundation of achievement. Did you measure up on the current standardized test? Will your test scores get you into the college of your choice? Are you getting the grades that prove that you are a cut above the others? It seems that success is based on how well you can compete in the race to rise above everyone around you. You are encouraged to be a go-getter rather than a go-giver. How does compassion fit in?

Compassion starts with yourself. You are human; you will fail; you will fall; you will falter along your way. "Pick yourself up and dust yourself off," as the song lyric goes. Sometimes it may not be as easy as that. Don't lose heart. Being compassionate is one way to keep your heart open and that will take some courage. It will take courage to travel on the road to awareness. It is an attribute that will keep you on course. Courage comes from the French word *coeur*, or heart. It takes heart to have courage, and heart to have compassion.

Try Doing Tonglen

There is a Buddhist exercise called *Tonglen* that is used for developing a compassionate heart. This is the way it works:

- When you experience any kind of pain, breathe into that pain on the in-breath.

- As you are doing that, think about how others on the planet may be experiencing that same pain at that very same moment.

- On the out-breath, exhale compassion, healing, or strength for yourself and all others who may be feeling similarly.

- It's breathing in mercy for many and breathing out healing for all.

Here's Another Exercise for You to Try

When you are feeling dark inside, you can fill your body with light.

- Close your eyes and slowly relax by counting down from ten to one as we did in earlier exercises.

- See in your mind's eye that you can send light throughout your body.

- Start with your head, then your neck, then your chest, then your torso, your stomach, your butt, and all the way down into your legs. Let your whole body fill with light.

- Now see that light extending outside your body.

- Encase yourself in a bubble or circle of light.

- Extend that light to others.

- Open your eyes and maintain the circle of light and your ability to extend it to others.

I remember seeing a cartoon on TV as a child that showed a group of elfin characters bottling sunshine. As they worked they sang, "Sunshine, sunshine." There was also a group of gnomish characters in this cartoon who were very dark and who sang, "I don't want to be happy, I want to be sad." They chanted this way until the elves poured bottled sunshine down their throats.

It is very much like that with you. You stay sad, unhappy, gloomy, or dissatisfied because you give yourself permission to be that way. You can choose that way of being. Being happy *is* like drinking bottled sunshine. You manufacture your own happiness. Being happy is a choice. Lighten up. Drink in the light and send it to those gloomy parts. Then you will be in a better position to send it out, to let it shine on others. But first start with yourself. Having compassion for yourself is the most important element in this process.

Compassion may be a popular word to look up in dictionaries, but is it so popular a practice in the world today? Is there any room for compassion in our lives? We all are so busy trying to get ahead that taking time to consider the needs of others may be a detriment rather than a course of action that we would want to take along our paths. The popular thing to do is usually dictated by the latest fashions. What you buy, what you wear, what you eat, how you speak, and even how you move are very much influenced by the latest styles and trends. Take a look at what is fashionable right now. What's hanging in your closet? What shows do you watch on TV? What food chains do you prefer? What are the latest electronics you own? It is hard to avoid the influence that the latest fashion has on the choices you make.

What if compassion were the fashion? We marvel at the compassionate deeds of people like Mother Theresa, Nelson Mandela, Martin Luther King Jr., and the Dali Lama of Tibet, who currently lives in exile. Each one of them faced incredible hardships, overcame horrific circumstances, and still maintained their love, trust, and faith in humanity in the face of whatever obstacles they encountered. They are our role models. Each exemplifies what it means to be compassionate.

How can any of us live up to that standard? It takes courage to be compassionate. It takes courage to accept yourself. It takes courage to accept others. It takes courage to maintain your strength and resolve in the face of adversity. It takes courage to assist others in doing the same.

You are human. We are all human. There is no hiding it. Hold your head high. Breathe in the miracle that is life; breathe in the miracle that is you. Keep your eyes open and wide as you look around and see all the beauty around you. See the humanity of all those you encounter. They, too, are a part of all the wonders of this planet. They, too, have their highs and lows, their light and dark sides. Know you can breathe in the light and let it fill you with strength and power. You also have the ability to send that light out and let it shine on everyone and everything around you. You are your own beacon, illuminating your own path as you walk your road to awareness.

You will start to meet fellow travelers on this road who will share your adventures and be willing to offer assistance and guidance. Let compassion be the fashion on the road to awareness. This is an amazing time to be alive.

As the song says said, "It is the dawning of the age of Aquarius." Every age has had its dominant energy. The age of Capricorn brought in the era of agriculture. The age of Taurus was dominated by bull cults throughout the Middle East. And the age of Pisces was the beginning of the Christian influence, as Christ was considered the fisher of men.

Now we see the beginning of a very different time period. For those who can look to the stars and see the constellations appearing in the evening sky, or for those who get to see the constellations only in books or planetariums, the constellation of Aquarius is a curious one. It is not a figure of an animal, but that of a young man, a servant, a water bearer. This may be the time for those who are willing to serve, a time for those who are willing to ensure that there is pure water for all. It will take determination and compassion for all living things to make sure we all have pure water, sufficient topsoil, and other natural resources to sustain life on this planet. We will all have to become servants of the planet. We will have to serve one another and the earth's resources for all life to sustain into the future. Compassion for all living things will be the order of the day.

"If you want others to be happy, practice compassion. If you want to be happy, practice compassion."- *Dalai Lama*

CHAPTER 11

Where's the Magic?

Seeing the Magic in Science

Nothing is impossible; the word itself says I'm possible.

—*Audrey Hepburn*

When my brother was thirteen he looked up, saw an airplane, and was taken by the miracle that could allow something that size to fly. He thought he would like to find out as much as he could about the dynamics of flight that could create such a magical thing. He decided to dedicate himself to this pursuit at a very young age. He was good in math, and he developed this skill in the study of aeronautics. Later in life he became the General Manager of International Space Systems for General Electric. He knew at thirteen the path he wanted to take. What are your dreams, what are your interests, what delights you?

You are the executive director of your life, your own CEO. It is the best job you will ever have. Which direction will you take, what paths will you follow, what roads will open up for you? This all will unfold as you become more adept at channeling the energy that generates the opportunities that reveal themselves along your path. Whether in the form of people, places, things, money, ideas, knowledge, skills, obstacles, opportunities, or anything that opens up to you or confronts you along your path, all can be used as energy to move you forward. You are energy. You are comprised of the very substances that fire the stars. Your life course of connecting to, understanding, and becoming more aware of the intrinsic connection that we all have to the ultimate source of life-giving light is a magical quest. The exploration of the hidden connections between all things is the fundamental purpose of science and where real magic begins.

This exploration begins with appreciation and wonder. When you appreciate everything around you, you may begin to wonder about it. According to Merriam-Webster, *appreciation* means "judgment, evaluation; especially a favorable critical estimate; a sensitive awareness; recognition of aesthetic values; an expression of admiration, approval or gratitude; increase in value."

When you save money, you hope that it will appreciate, that it will grow in value. As with anything when we appreciate it, it will grow in value in our eyes, or in the eyes of others. *Appreciate* is a powerful verb. It is an action that allows you to increase the value of your resources, and gain benefit from what appears to you along your path. When you appreciate something it becomes valuable to you, you give it energy. All energy is like an electrical charge or current. You can infuse that energy or current into anything you see.

It is interesting that money is considered currency, because money is a form of energy. You have the ability to give value to whatever you wish by infusing it with your energy, your personal currency for growth. This can happen through your appreciation.

Wonder arises when you start to view your world and all that is in it with appreciation. *Wonder* is defined by Merriam-Webster as: "a cause of astonishment or admiration; a miracle; the quality of exciting amazed admiration; rapt attention or astonishment at something awesomely mysterious or new to one's experience; a feeling of doubt or uncertainty."

You can wonder at the wonder of something. Maybe what impels scientific exploration is wondering at the wonder. How much you want to explore is your prerogative. There is real wonder in science, and many miracles to explore.

We take the miracles that we see all around us every day for granted. The very fact that our body knows how to inhale the oxygen from the air and deliver it to the parts of the body where it is needed and then expel the waste of carbon dioxide is nothing short of miraculous. Our atmosphere, in its marvelous blue hue, keeps us safe from harmful radiation. These are things we cannot take lightly. Miracles are all around us in every moment of every day. You are a part of that miraculous harmony, as is every other creature on this planet, as is every other element that comprises this amazing world. When you can stand in awe of the beautiful being that you are among the glory that is in this world, you begin to see that everything you are is a part of that ongoing miracle.

You can connect to the wisdom of the universe by quieting the chatter in your mind, slowing down, and allowing for the stillness that comes when you allow yourself to be fully present. There is a wisdom in the universe—some call it the collective unconscious—like an underground spring that dwells within you that can provide guidance. Stilling your mind, stilling the confusion and chatter that sometimes befuddles you, and taking time to listen to the messages within yourself can provide opportunities to connect to that wisdom.

There is harmony in the universe. It was when Beethoven became totally deaf that he was able to compose his greatest works. It may have been at that point he was able to truly listen to the universal harmonies. The universe operates in a wonderful harmonious dance. Planets revolve around the sun, and our moon revolves around the earth in a perfectly balanced dance. I remember looking up at the moon through a telescope during a total lunar eclipse and marveling at the big gray rock that is suspended so precariously in the sky when not illuminated by the sun. "It's just a big rock," I thought. "Thank God it doesn't fall on us." We are blessed by the miracle that keeps the moon suspended above our planet and allows the light of the sun to shine on it so beautifully every night.

It is a challenge to express what you can care about rather than what you can complain about. Your care taps you into an awareness of what works and what doesn't, while complaining does little to resolve or solve anything. That doesn't mean you won't make mistakes. In fact, sometimes it is important to fail in order to redirect and rediscover a better avenue of approach.

My brother told a story about working with a Japanese scientist to develop a satellite surveillance system that could penetrate the depths of the deepest oceans. Their efforts were a failure, and the managers of the Japanese company supporting the project considered it a disgrace that my brother and the Japanese engineers had failed. My brother had a different perspective about this failure. He believed that without failure there can be no innovation. You must be willing to fail. Failure is not a stop. It is just a beginning, a detour, a minor roadblock in the discovery process.

Wonder starts with saying, "I don't know." If you had all the answers, where would the fun of exploration lie? Not knowing is a wonderful place to begin any journey. It is also a necessary starting point when looking at ways to solve problems, discover solutions, fix mistakes, or overcome obstacles. It is very often the inability to admit to not knowing that keeps you stuck in unsuccessful patterns. Allowing for the perspective of not knowing the answer to something may open up new realms of possibility for success.

What role does science play in our lives? What is the purpose of scientific study? Is it to harness and control nature so we can better use the resources of nature? Or does science allow us to better understand our place in the great harmonious scheme of the universe? In the name of progress and greater productivity, some companies are developing techniques to better extract nonrenewable resources from the earth, develop agricultural techniques, or engineer foods that increase production. These very techniques can be damaging to the planet, deplete the soil, and can be harmful to your health. Other companies are looking for ways to enhance a more sustainable way for all humans to live peacefully and harmoniously on Earth. President Correa of Ecuador recently made an appeal to the developed nations of the world who use the greater percentage of the earth's resources, and subsequently contribute the most to the destruction of the biosphere, to contribute to the support and preservation of the rain forest. Asking for billions to support this effort, he received only millions in response. This amount will not be enough for his country to protect the rain forest from exploitation. Protecting and preserving the rain forest is vital for the survival of the planet. The rain forest's role in oxygen generation, the hidden secrets of the medicinal components of its exotic and healing plants, as well as the splendor and magic of the animal species that inhabit this region must be protected. Science can be used to develop or destroy. The pursuit of science is a journey along a razor's edge. Its direction will determine whether we get in our future a paradise lost or a paradise reclaimed. Eden is now; it is all around us. What can we do to protect it? What role do you want to play?

While I was studying for my masters degree at Northwestern, I had the opportunity to work with a group of middle school students in Calumet, Indiana, at the local PBS station. We worked on creating a TV show called *Beware! We're Aware!* The purpose of this show was for the students to explore and compare the meaning of opposites such as freedom and responsibility, arrogance and humility, hate and love, joy and sorrow, or peace and aggression. The students created skits and animations and conducted interviews with experts in order to show that young people are quite capable of understanding important issues that affect how they can better understand themselves, their world, and their place in it. Young people just like yourself are capable of exploring complex problems, whether they be scientific or philosophical, just as the students at Beach Channel High School did in helping the park rangers and Coast Guard clean up Jamaica Bay.

My son had a great expression that I always loved. He told me he was "meant to invent." What will you invent? What will you create? What new vistas will you explore? What might you discover?

Try These for Yourself

Here are some ideas from Margo Mullein, founder of Walking Root Healing, Herbs, Gardens.

Create a vision and dream journal: Everyone dreams, both while awake (of what they would like to see in their lives, aka visions) and when they are sleeping (those wonderful messages from the dream world). It's a process in which you will discover much about yourself. Making a collage is both creative and easy—an art form that anyone can do! You will need a bunch of favorite magazines, a composition book (a notebook), and some white glue. Scissors are optional. (I like to just tear mine out.)

- Leaf through the pages of the magazine, thinking about places you dream of visiting, things you would like to have some day, favorite things that mean a lot to you, and so on.

- Cut out the things that catch your eye, whether they be persons, places, things, or even words. Once you have a good collection, start to assemble them on your page. You can collage both the front and back of your vision and dream journal. You can make one side represent the you in the here and now, and the other side a future you. You can dedicate one side to your sleeping dreams, and the other to the visions that you have during your (awake) life. Just remember that to everything you cut out of the magazine and paste into your journal you are giving your energy and setting an intention for its meaning, purpose, and fruition.

Things I am good at: Make a top ten list of things you are really good at. Take your time with this one, as if you were doing it as a meditation. Sit in a quiet space where you will not be disturbed. Create a relaxing atmosphere by lighting a candle, playing some soft music, or anything else that comes to mind that will put you into the mood to focus on y-o-u! Have a pen and paper (or perhaps your vision and dream journal, if you made one).

- One by one, taking your time, giving it careful thought, list ten things that you are really good at.

- Once you have written ten things, take a deep breath (to bring it all in) and then read the list out loud, beginning with the words "I am really good (or great) at ..." Again, take your time with this. This is you celebrating you, and you deserve all the time in the world!

· Once you have read your list out loud, skip a few lines and write five things that you would like to be really good at. Remember, the sky's the limit. Just as you did with your top ten, read the list beginning with the words "I would like to be really good (or great) at …"

· Once you have completed this, go to the bottom of your list and identify two people from your school, home, or community who you can talk to about achieving these five new gifts you would like to give yourself. Make a commitment to get in touch with them, and tell them of your desire. When you do, ask if they would be willing to mentor or guide you through that process.

Identify a tree in your yard, on your street, or at a favorite park. Make sure it is located in a place that you can visit frequently, as this project is one where you will observe this tree during each of the four seasons. Your objective will be to record your observations through sketching, painting, journaling, writing, photography, or prose.

· Reflect on the shape; see if you can notice anything about its energy. (Does it look like a happy, or perhaps a sad tree?) Does it have buds? Or full leaves? What is the pattern of the branches, and of the bark along the trunk of the tree?

· Do you see any birds who are enjoying this tree? What about insects? What do you notice about where it is growing, and do you have any sense of the tree's relationship to that space?

· This is a four-season exercise, and the tree will transform itself each season. Each season, see if you can notice anything about where the tree is located that mirrors something within your own life.

· Here is an important detail to this exercise: While you are with the tree, recording your observations in whichever method you decide (and you can pick a different method during each season if you wish), breathe deeply. With each breath in, think about how you are breathing in thanks to the oxygen that the tree has produced. With each breath out, think about how you are providing the carbon dioxide that the tree breathes in. With each breath, connect to the important relationship and balance between tree and human.

- At the end of your tree observation, take a few moments to contemplate the experience and the feelings that come up for you during this exercise. Find some way that feels natural to you to thank the tree for sharing its time with you. I often just touch the tree or simply say, "Thank you." Other times, I might sing it a song, or even give it a hug. However you choose to acknowledge the exchange, let it come from your heart.

Some Other Things You Might Want to Do

- Write an article for your school newspaper about an issue that concerns you.

- Write an editorial for a local paper. Your voice is important.

- Write to your congressman about an issue that confuses or bothers you, about how our political system is handling or not handling something of concern in your community.

- Start a club. The 4-H Club is particularly popular in rural environments. What about the possibility of a 5-H Club in which you explore: Health, Harmony, Happiness, Honor and Humor?

CHAPTER 12

Commencement

Sharing My Contribution on the Road to Awareness

Remember happiness is a way of travel, not a destination.

—Roy Goodman

If you have journeyed this far, you are well along your way on the road to awareness. You have determined your own course, you are aware of your resources, you know the pitfalls, and your roadmaps and road signs are in place. You understand that you can direct your own energy as a beacon in the night, lighting your own way. You have everything you need to succeed. You might consider yourself a traveling light who travels light.

Take your time on the road to awareness. Observe what appears along the way. Beware of categorizing anything as negative or positive. Consider everything you encounter as energy currency for your use to stay on course. Don't let anything capture you or deter you from your own progress. Acknowledge the presence of obstacles as opportunities and carry on. Observe, check out patterns, take time to delight in the energy, and use it all to propel you. Enjoy the people you meet along the way. Relish and appreciate them. They are possible partners in your quest.

Look for the value in your encounters, and determine what is valuable to you. Go for the gold, but remember that all that glitters is not gold. Where will you find value? Where will you put value? Will it be on your inherent qualities and personal virtues? Will it be love, compassion, kindness, contribution, and the quality of your character that add to the value of your life?

Where does the journey take you? Ultimately, it takes you to *love*. My own journey has been marked by appreciation and wonder, as well as hurt and despair. I am well aware of the times when continuing to get up and brush myself off seemed more than I could bear. I also know that reaching for the energy that can pull you through difficult times can sometimes bring you to new and challenging vistas you never before imagined. Have faith that life and all its energy is a wonder to explore. Let that exploration delight your curiosity.

The late Princess Diana was very concerned about the mine fields that were left in Bosnia after the civil war there. Children would play in those fields unsuspecting of any danger. One step on the mines would cost a limb or a life. Before her death she helped to draw attention to mine-clearing operations. Her efforts helped to influence the passage of the Ottawa Treaty, which created an international ban on the use of land mines.

You will encounter such hazards in the form of *mind fields*. Maneuvering your way around certain individuals who may want to tap your energy, rob you of your sense of self, dissuade you from your personal power, or keep you from achieving success can be like walking through a field of mines. Trust yourself and protect your boundaries. You may experience hurt, anger, betrayal, or pain. Just like Harry Potter was given the invisibility cloak by his parents to conceal himself when necessary, know that you can put on a cloak of peace that will soothe your weary soul when needed.

Life's journey can present hazards as well as happiness. You may feel scared by some of the things you encounter. Initially it may be difficult to discern the good from the bad. Everything is a bonus on the road of life when you see it as part of the sacred energy of the universe. You can change *scared* to *sacred* by flipping the second and third letters of those words. When you are scared, you are caught by those emotions that can hold you back. When you are moving into the sacred, you are in action to make the most of everything you see before you.

Try This On

· Imagine a cloak of peace made out of soft, fluffy material much like a robe or cloak worn by a king or queen.

· The cloak is hooded and can cover your head, and feels very soft around you.

· Mentally put it on when you need protection.

· Let it calm your fears, your hurts, and your pain.

· Walk tall as a king or queen protected by your cloak of peace.

· Let it help you settle into your own personal power so that you always know the appropriate direction to take for yourself.

Behind? Below? Which way should you go? There will be many roads to follow, and many places to go. Don't let the road signs that say Stop, Do Not Enter, Yield, and Wrong Way deter you. Look for the *right of way* for yourself. When I was a member of the Actors Experimental Unit in New York, I wrote a musical play for children called *Behind, Below? Which Way Should I Go?* This play was written as an inner space fantasy. One song, written by Susan Moss for that play, was called "My Sky." A bird that was being pushed out of the nest by its mother began to sing on first experiencing flight:

Oh, my goodness, how can this be?

What is happening to me?

I am flying, flying high in my sky.

The little girl character who witnessed the baby bird's first flight replied:

> If that bird can fly so gracefully,
>
> I can travel any road I see.
>
> Flying is up to me.

To be peaceful, you have to see peace, and to see peace you have to expect peace. Your perceptions create the projections of what you see and what you experience in your world. All everyone wants is respect. You can give everyone you meet *Ra*-spect, as in the ancient Egyptian sun god Ra. You can offer respect to each person you meet in the form of light as from the sun. You may not agree with everyone. You don't have to be disagreeable to disagree. However, you can certainly send anyone and everyone light so that they can see more clearly through their own darkness. Your ability to conjure the presence of light within yourself can be a source of stability and power.

When I was feeling the most discouraged, I wrote this poem that I would like to share. Because of all I experienced, I am very certain that my path is one of love. Maybe you would like to write your own poem.

A Return to Love

> Love to create, generate, appreciate;
>
> Expand to give to those you deem to love.
>
> Banned, barred, cast away,
>
> Shunned, robbed of what is most precious,
>
> Cut off, expelled, left without …
>
> Now
>
> Hurt, pain, fear of rejection,
>
> Sorrow, alone, hopeless,
>
> Harmed, no way back.

Yet

A glimmer of light,

Internalized power

Pulled from the depths

Of the limitless mercy.

Energy, grace, joy, delight,

A step on the path

That returns home to

Love.

How About Trying This?

The broadcasting students at Beach Channel, Edward R. Murrow, and Jacqueline Kennedy Onassis were given the assignment to create a public service announcement (PSA) about an issue that they thought was important for the public to know. A PSA on either television or radio is a thirty-second ad offered free of charge. Broadcast stations are required to air PSAs as part of their licensing agreement to protect the public interest. Students were very creative in addressing issues they thought affected their peers. What problems concern you? How would you use television or radio to inform your peers about them?

Try These

- Draw a picture about what is important to you.

- Take a photograph that expresses your concerns.

- Make up an action hero to solve problems you see affecting teens.

- Draw a cartoon.

- Create a comic book.

- Devise a better world campaign.

Enjoy your journey. No one has gone on your path before, and no one ever will repeat the journey you are about to embark. You will see wonders along the way when you take a moment to appreciate all the small and large miracles in your life.

NOTES

Introduction

Kathleen M. Galvin and Casandra Book, *Person to Person: An Introduction to Speech Communication, 5ʰ Edition* (National Textbook company, 1994). This is the textbook that I used for the Interpersonal Communication classes at Beach Channel High School. It is a wonderful text for teens. It takes you through lessons and exercises so that you can better understand yourself as a communicator, to understanding yourself when communicating one-on-one, in small group settings, or when addressing larger groups.

Chapter 1

Merriam-Webster's Collegiate Dictionary, 11ʰ Edition (Springfield: Merriam-Webster, Inc., 2004), 86. Using the dictionary was an important part of all my classes. I got this lesson from John Sexton when he taught our SAT prep class at St. Brendan's High School when I was a teen. He said that every word you learn is a dollar in the bank.

For more information about the Silva Life System, please check out their website www.silvalifesystem.com.

Chapter 2

Luigi Pirandello, *Six Characters In Search of an Author* (New York: Penguin Books, 1995).

Merriam-Webster's Collegiate Dictionary, 11th Edition (Springfield: Merriam-Webster, Inc., 2004), 420.

Merriam-Webster's Collegiate Dictionary, 11th Edition (Springfield: Merriam-Webster, Inc., 2004), 898.

Edward R. Murrow High School was designated a School of Excellence by the United States Department of Education. For more information about the school, go to their website www.ermurrow.org. The school provides students the opportunity to grow in an environment of structured freedom.

Chapter 3

Dr. Joe Dispenza, *Breaking the Habit of Being Yourself: How to Lose Your Mind and Create a New One* (Carlsbad, California: Hay House, Inc., 2012).

Dr. Masaru Emoto, David A. Thoyne (translator), *The Hidden Messages of Water* (Hillsboro: Beyond Words Publishing, Inc., 2004).

Deepak Chopra, *Power, Freedom and Grace: Living from the Source of Lasting Happiness* (San Rafael: Amber-Allen Publishers, 2006), 55–56.

Chapter 5

T.H. Whyte, *Once and Future King* (New York: The Berkley Publishing Group, Inc., 1987).

Chapter 6

John Neihardt, *Black Elk Speaks* (Lincoln: University of Nebraska Press, 1993).

Frederick W. Turner III (editor), *The Portable North American Indian Reader* (New York: Viking Press, 1986).

Hyemeyohsts Storm, *Seven Arrows* (New York: Ballantine Books, 1972).

Dee Brown, *Bury My Heart at Wounded Knee* (New York: Bantam books, 1976).

Chapter 7

Chinua Achebe, *Things Fall Apart* (New York: Ballantine Books, 1959). The title *Things Fall Apart* is taken from the poem "The Second Coming," by William Butler Yeats.

Merriam-Webster's Collegiate Dictionary, 11th Edition (Springfield: Merriam-Webster, Inc., 2004), 417.

Merriam-Webster's Collegiate Dictionary, 11th Edition (Springfield: Merriam-Webster, Inc., 2004), 1060.

Chapter 8

John Michael Tebelak (book) and Stephen Schwartz (music and lyrics), *Godspell*. Based on the Gospel according to St. Matthew, *Godspell* was first produced at the Cherry Lane Theatre in New York in 1971. *Godspell* was John Michael Tebelak's masters thesis at Carnegie Mellon University in 1970. Music Theatre International in New York holds the rights for theatrical performances.

Chapter 10

Merriam-Webster's Collegiate Dictionary, 11th Edition (Springfield: Merriam-Webster, Inc., 2004), 253.

Chapter 11

Merriam-Webster's Collegiate Dictionary, 11th Edition (Springfield: Merriam-Webster, Inc., 2004), 61.

Merriam-Webster's Collegiate Dictionary, 11th Edition (Springfield: Merriam-Webster, Inc., 2004), 1440.

You can contact Margo Mullein of Walking Root at <walkingroot@gmail.com>

Chapter 12

J.K. Rowling, *Harry Potter and the Philosopher's Stone: Year One at Hogwarts* (London: Bloomsbury Press, 1997).

J.K. Rowling, *Harry Potter and the Sorcerer's Stone: Year One at Hogwarts* (New York: Scholastic Corporation, 1998).

ABOUT THE AUTHOR

 Barbara Abbate has over thirty years of experience in classrooms around the country. She was a teacher, playwright, and director for the American Conservatory Theatre's Young Conservatory in San Francisco. She was instrumental in the creation of Beach Channel High School, the magnet school of oceanography, the director of the broadcasting programs at Edward R. Murrow High School, and at Jacqueline Kennedy Onassis High School in New York City. She was honored as a MetLife Teaching Fellow through Impact II Teachers Network, and as a Master Teacher by Rutgers University.

Currently, Barbara creates *Awareness High School* to inspire young people, teachers, and parents to take the reins of their own educational development and seek out alternative ways to learn.

Ms. Abbate is retired and currently living in Austin, Texas. Please contact Barbara Abbate on her website awarenesshighschool.com or barbaraabbate.com to share and learn about other opportunities along the road to awareness.

Printed in the United States
By Bookmasters